REPAIRING THE BREACH

Ministering in Community Conflict

Ronald S. Kraybill

HERALD PRESS
Scottdale, Pennsylvania
Kitchener, Ontario

82 83 84 85 86 87 88 12 11 10 9 8 7 6 5 4 3

Contents

Foreword

Recent years have seen growing interest in alternative means for resolving disputes. Particularly exciting has been the keen interest among church people across the religious spectrum in ministries of reconciliation. Many more than those within the so-called "peace churches" hear the call to live the "Gospel of peace"!

As director of a program recently established by the Peace Section of Mennonite Central Committee to support involvement of churches in the ministry of peace, I have become keenly aware of the scarcity of written materials in this field. Peacemakers have learned much in recent years and continue to learn much about helpful responses to community conflict. But there have been few attempts to consolidate this learning. The time is here to tell stories, to share experiences, and make available to others what the practitioners are learning.

Motivated more by a sense of the urgent need to begin filling this gap than by an abundance of expertise, I have undertaken the task of presenting in this book things I have learned or observed in recent years. Others with more experience than I will readily see the limitations in what follows. Yet I trust the journeymen will not judge this apprentice too bold for attempting imperfectly what they have been too busy to undertake.

* * * * * * *

One lesson I have learned from involvement in conflict is that if those who are called to peacemaking wait for security in their role, they never begin. Not that the ministry of reconciliation is unrewarding. Quite the contrary. There are even moments of glory. But I will confess that after involvement in quite a few human tangles, it is still a rare dispute that fails to arouse feelings of vulnerability and uncertainty in me.

Another lesson I am learning is fortitude. There are no short-cuts in peacemaking. Yes, competence helps, but perseverance in the midst of the unknown and the unpromising is equally important. To make peace is not only to be vulnerable, but to hold fast and embrace the experience of personal weakness.

The unique gift that accompanies the calling, however, is the dawning realization that weakness need neither intimidate nor paralyze. Partly through faith, partly through practice, I have come to see that vulnerability and weakness are inherent in all that holds promise of life.

Through faith, because all that is eternal in Christianity begins with worldly weakness and apparent failure. Why do Christians struggle so for the marks of success?

Through practice, because awareness of vulnerability is the starting point for all genuine communication. When I face and accept my own vulnerability, I am free to listen to others and to experience the power of love. When I understand the vulnerability of others, they can find the freedom to listen in return. Love which is gladly vulnerable often opens a way through the multitude of defenses present in conflict.

Can it be that vulnerability and weakness are not at all fearsome enemies, but rather constitute the Christian peacemaker's franchise to ministry?

Ronald S. Kraybill, Director
Mennonite Conciliation Service
Mennonite Central Committee U.S.
Akron, Pennsylvania

I / The Bible on Reconciliation

I. Introduction

"Glory to God in the highest and on earth peace, good will, towards men."

Perhaps the most over-looked word in history is the *and* pronounced by the angels when Jesus was born. How much easier to obey one half of the mandate or the other! To lift solemn ceremony to God and evade responsibility to work for peace among men. Or equally tempting, to struggle for human perfection and ignore the Creator.

Most Christians hear only the first half of the angels' words. Like the children of Israel, we are inclined to believe that mainly our Maker craves an attitude of praise or an impressive display of worship among his children.

Not that we don't have a place for peace. Christians talk, to be sure, a great deal about peace. Popular Christianity of the radio and TV variety, and much Christian literature today are full of words of peace. "When peace like a river ascendeth my way...," we sing. And we testify glowingly of "peace with God" or peace in our souls.

Nothing wrong with peace with God. I value mine highly! The problem is that peace as it is used by many Christians today does not mean what it normally means in Scripture. Peace today in Christian circles frequently describes a purely individual, highly subjective experience that is only a shadow of the biblical meaning. Peace is inner calm, tranquility, good feelings, the quiet conscience that follows when God has released a sinner from guilt.

Without a doubt, peace in this narrow sense is an important part of Christian experience. But if this is the extent of the peace the angels promised, Christianity offers little more than the latest relaxation technique marketed on every streetcorner today. I know *non*-Christian meditators boasting lower pulse rates than many Christians. If inner quietude was his aim, surely Jesus would have fixed a sure-fire relaxation technique somewhere in the early verses of the Sermon on the Mount!

Granted, Christians do not always speak of peace so narrowly. "We ought to pray for world peace" is a statement many Christians would agree with, meaning peace among nations. But even here, Christians rarely use the word with the sense of urgency attached to it in Scripture. Peace concerns Christians as it concerns all good citizens, but it is a secondary concern, a calling peripheral to the core of the Gospel. Establishing peace where prejudice, conflict, and injustice reign are viewed as significant deeds, but they are not integral to Christ's saving work on the cross. Peacemaking occurs *after* proclamation of the message, not as an inseparable part of the message itself.

The result is a loss in vitality of the message itself. Remove the concept of peacemaking from proclaiming the Gospel and the very meaning of Gospel changes. The Good News becomes something that can be *said* without doing, talked about and believed, without being lived and acted upon. The Gospel heals hearts, not relationships. As a result, proclamation suffers. No longer can observers say, "See how they love!" but only "Hear how happy they say they are!"

To summarize, how we understand peace, and what we do with the Bible's call to peace, influence us in areas that most Christians agree are crucial to our faith. That is, our understanding of salvation and openness to receiving it, our life as a church, and our mission activities—all are directly linked to how we deal with the theme of reconciliation in the Bible.

II. Shalom in the Old Testament

The beginning point for examining the theme of reconciliation in the Bible is the Old Testament word *shalom*, the Hebrew word normally translated as "peace". Found over 300 times in the Old Testament, shalom occupies a broad plane of meaning and appears in many contexts, ranging from casual greetings to covenants between God and his people.

Shalom is an expansive term. It describes much more than "absence of conflict" and points far beyond subjective inward personal experience. Shalom describes an entire state of well-being, health, happiness, material security, harmony with neighbors, justice, economic equality, and spiritual integrity.

One can observe the following about shalom in the Old Testament.

1) Shalom is central to God's intentions for human existence—where earthly pens are straining to phrase God's deep desire for His creatures, there the word *shalom* appears. (Num. 6:24-26; Lev. 26:3-10; Jer. 29:10-11; Ps. 34:14.)
2) Shalom and "salvation" are virtually synonymous. (Ps. 85:5ff; Ps. 119:165; Is. 32.)
3) Shalom is found in relation to others; in seeking their well-being. (Jer. 29:7; Ps. 34:14.)
4) Shalom includes *justice* and God's children are to take an active hand in maintaining it. (Is. 32:16-17; Jer. 6:14; 8:11.)
5) Shalom is more important to God than solemn worship. (Is. 58:1-12; Amos 5:21-24.)

6) God's new covenant will be a "covenant of shalom." (Ez. 37:26, 27; Is. 2:2-4; Micah 4:1-4.) God's suffering servant will be "Prince of Shalom." (Is. 6:9.)

For additional study, see "Shalom and Christ" in *The Predicament of the Prosperous* by Bruce Birch and L. Rasmussen (Westminster, 1978) or James Metzler's essay "Shalom is the Mission" in *Mission and the Peace Witness*, edited by Robert Ramseyer (Herald Press, 1979).

Several points deserve special emphasis for Christians today. For one, shalom is central to salvation in the Old Testament. It is a primary goal for God's children, not a secondary, optional task. Secondly, shalom is a condition occurring in relationships with other humans, not merely in the individual heart. Naturally, the decision to participate in God's intentions is made in the heart of the individual. But the focus quickly moves outward. The meaning and the real test of the decision is experienced especially in the realm of human relationships.

Thirdly, God expects His children to participate in the effort to create and maintain shalom. Indeed, active commitment to shalom is viewed as a definitive test of obedience (see #4 and #5 above); where God's people neglect the ministry of shalom, God is wrathful or totally absent. Finally, I consider it important in understanding the teachings of Christ to note that shalom in the Old Testament is limited to God's covenant people— thus the occasional startling contrasts between calls to shalom and calls to war against those outside the covenant.

III. Jesus as Bringer of Shalom

The Old Testament points to shalom as the expression of God's desire for His redeemed people. The prophets look ahead to the Messiah and a coming time of shalom.

Consistent with the direction of these traditions, the New Testament offers ample evidence to suggest that Jesus and others around Him shared the vision. That is, bringing shalom, in the full Old Testament meaning of the term, was the heart of Jesus' mission.

A. *The expectations of others awaiting his birth describe Jesus in terms characteristic of the vision of shalom.* Of the four Gospels, only Luke devotes major attention to the expectations of those awaiting Jesus. Appearing in Luke's account is the firm conviction that Jesus will introduce a reversal of social and spiritual conditions which could only be described as a state of shalom in the broad-reaching, concrete Old Testament sense of the word.

Mary rejoices in the coming deliverer who "has exalted those of low degree and has filled the hungry with good things, and the rich he has sent empty away." (Lk. 1:52-53.) Zechariah looks forward to delivery from the hand of enemies who would oppress (Lk. 1:73-75), and who would "guide our feet into the way of peace." And John the Baptist asserts that the way to respond to the Messiah is to share possessions, and to deal honestly and kindly in relations with others. (Lk. 3:10-14.)

B. *Jesus introduced himself as the bringer of the Old Testament vision of shalom.* Jesus' words at his first public appearance at the Nazareth temple were clear and disturbing to his audience: "The Spirit of the Lord is upon me, because he has anointed me to preach good news to the poor. He has sent me to proclaim release to the captives and recovering of sight to the blind, to set at liberty those who are oppressed, to proclaim the acceptable year of the Lord." (Lk. 4:18-19.) On that day, Jesus informed his listeners, those ancient words of prophecy were fulfilled.

C. *Jesus' life was a ministry of shalom.* Surely it is unnecessary to document in detail the way in which Jesus' life cohered with his proclamation of the vision of shalom. His ministry focused largely on *healing,* a concrete act of bringing wholeness to others. He counted his friends mainly among those despised by the rest of society. He emphasized service to others and love of enemies. He often instructed sinners that the first act of repentance is righting relations with others. He taught that the telling question in the Final Judgment will be whether his followers have fed the hungry, clothed the naked, housed the homeless. Perhaps most telling, Jesus demonstrated love which sacrifices self to proclaim God's kingdom of shalom.

In Jesus, the call to repentance and the ministry of shalom are inseparable. Repentance is not genuine unless there is commitment to shalom. And the mission of shalom is empty unless there is repentance, turning from self to God and others.

To the end, Jesus testified to the kingdom now beginning, where worshipping God and reconciling the enemy even at personal expense are inseparable acts. Death itself could not separate these in the life of Christ.

IV. Reconciliation in the Early Church

Perhaps the most persuasive biblical evidence for understanding Jesus' life and teachings as a call to ministries of reconciliation is the unmistakable emphasis of the early church on reconciliation. Sociologically and theologically, it is clear that those closest to the life of Christ took the task of reconciliation with utmost seriousness.

A. *Reconciling Jew and Gentile was a primary concern in the early church.* The New Testament church spent enormous time and energy struggling to make reconciliation between Jew and Gentile a reality in their midst. Jewish Christians especially undertook this commitment at great expense—loss of certain Jewish religious traditions, as well as ostracism by family and friends. The book of Acts reverberates with the struggle—there is no explaining the perseverance of the early church in this struggle unless they were convinced that reconciliation between the two peoples was central to the meaning of Christ.

B. *New Testament authors repeatedly present the nature of God and*

Christ in terms of reconciliation. Various New Testament writers refer to God as "the God of peace" (Rom. 15:33; 16:20; II Cor. 13:11; Phil. 4:9; Heb. 13:20; I Thes. 5:23), describe Jesus as "Lord of peace" (Eph. 2:14ff; II Thes. 3:16; Heb. 7:2), and the Gospel as the "Gospel of peace" (Acts 10:36; Rom. 10:15; Eph. 6:15).

C. *The Apostle Paul presents a "theology of reconciliation."* Paul reflects frequently on the meaning of Christ in his writings to a church still struggling to articulate the significance of the incredible events surrounding Jesus' life and death. The theme of reconciliation—between God and humans, between one human and another— is dominant in the thought of this first prominent Christian theologian.

Consider the following three passages in which Paul interprets the work of Christ:

"For in him all the fulness of God was pleased to dwell, and through him to reconcile to himself all things, whether on earth or in heaven, making peace by the blood of his cross. And you, who once were estranged and hostile in mind, doing evil deeds, he has now reconciled in his body of flesh by his death, in order to present you holy and blameless and irreproachable before him." (Col. 1:19-22.)

"Therefore, if anyone is in Christ, he is a new creation; the old has passed away, behold, the new has come. All this is from God, who through Christ reconciled us to himself and gave us the ministry of reconciliation; that is, God was in Christ reconciling the world to himself, not counting their trespasses against them and entrusting to us the message of reconciliation. So we are ambassadors for Christ, God making his appeal through us." (II Cor. 5:17-20a.)

"But now in Christ Jesus you who once were far off have been brought near in the blood of Christ. For he is our peace, who has made us both one, and has broken down the dividing wall of hostility, by abolishing in his flesh the law of commandments and ordinances, that he might create in himself one new man in place of the two, so making peace, and might reconcile us *both* to God in one body through the cross, thereby bringing the hostility to an end. And he came and preached peace to you who were far off and peace to those who were near." (Eph. 2:13-17.)

The concept common to all three of these passages is Christ as Reconciler. Christ reconciles the world to himself, reconciles humans to one another, and has committed to the church the ministry of reconciliation.

Now, this talk of reconciliation sounds very human. It this a departure from grace, an attempt to place the burden of salvation on human action? No— Paul makes clear the source of our salvation. "All of this is from God, who through Christ reconciled us to himself, and gave us the ministry of

11

reconciliation." (II Cor. 5:18.) Clearly the ministry of reconciliation among humans does not itself save; it is rather the first fruit of salvation.

The key is this: Salvation brings a new creation in Christ. Paul wrote, "You have put off the old nature with its practices and have put on the new nature, which is being renewed after the image of the Creator. Here there cannot be Greek and Jew, circumcised and uncircumcised, barbarian, Scythian, slave, free man, but Christ is all, and in all." (Col. 3:10-11; cf: I Cor. 12-13; Gal. 3:28.) This phrase, "Neither Jew nor Greek, male nor female..." is a formula Paul uses repeatedly to describe the earthly result of salvation, the visible characteristics of the redeemed. Reconciliation among humans is the identifying mark of God's new creation!

But for Paul that is not the end of it. It is not enough simply to *be reconciled*—the church is called to undertake the task of reconciliation. "All this is from God, who through Christ reconciled us to himself and gave us the ministry of reconciliation." (II Cor. 5:18.) Because we are reconciled, we are called to be reconcilers.

V. Reconciliation: The Agenda For Today

If indeed the call to reconciling ministries is central to the Bible's message, what are the implications for Christians seeking to be faithful to God's intentions? Obedience to the Biblical witness requires re-examination, I believe, both of the church's self-understanding in relation to disputes among believers, as well as of the church's understanding of mission.

A. Conflict Ministries: The Heart of Church Life

The Apostle Paul had strong words to offer on disputes within the church. The force of his writings on this question makes sense only when we understand that the concept of reconciliation was crucial to Paul's understanding of salvation in Christ. Despite the diversity of members, the church is *one* body in Christ, he writes in I Corinthians 12. Disputes within the church threaten unity in Christ, he asserts, thus weakening what we have seen is the primary evidence of Christ's saving power. Resolution of disputes among believers, then, is a matter of first-rate ecclesiastical significance.

Interestingly, Paul is not so much concerned about the existence of the disputes among Christians, as he is with *how* disputes are resolved. In Galatians 6 and Philippians 4, for example, Paul does not scold for disagreements. Rather, he merely make direct requests for appointment of mediators, "yokefellows" as he calls them in Philippians 4:3. A similar pattern appears in I Corinthians 6, where Paul is matter-of-fact about the existence of disagreements in the church. What disturbs Paul—and his anger is scathing—is that Christians are taking disputes to secular courts instead of resolving them with the help of Christian mediators. "How dare you go to law before the unrighteous instead of the saints? Can it be that there is no man among you wise enough to decide between members of the brotherhood...?" (I Cor. 6:1-7.) The church is to provide a forum for resolving

12

disputes *within* the fellowship of believers.

Paul is not developing novel ideas here, but rather articulates teachings already familiar from the tradition of Jesus' words recorded in Matthew 18. Many Christians today are acquainted with the formula for resolving disputes recorded in Matthew 18. Less recognized is that Jesus placed this dispute settlement process at the heart of the church's function. That is, Jesus called the process "binding and loosing" (Mt. 18:15-20), his phrase for the exercise of church authority (cf: Mt. 16:13-20), and stated that it has eternal significance. Interestingly, only in these two passages dealing with conflict and authority is the word "church" ever reported on the lips of Jesus.

The greatest misunderstanding of Matthew 18 today occurs in the frequent abuse of verse 20, where Jesus promised that "Where two or three are gathered together in my name, there am I in the midst of them." Modern readers usually take this as a mandate for small prayer meetings.

Examination of the context leaves no room for this interpretation—the whole chapter is focused on relationships and misunderstandings and this verse clearly is linked to that theme! Moreover, "two or three gathered" is a phrase familiar from Old Testament usage in the context of adjudicating disputes; it indicates an acceptable quorum of witnesses. (Cf: Dt. 17:6; 19:15; Heb. 10:28; *et al.*) Thus it seems clear that Jesus' words are intended for peacemakers. Where believers gather to resolve disputes in his name, Christ is present among them.

In summary, Paul's attention to disputes, and the strength of his words on this topic arise from a source deeper than the concern that any leader would naturally have for harmony within the flock. Paul understood, for one, that Christ came to reconcile. Reconciliation is the primary mark of redemption. Then too, Paul undoubtedly drew from the tradition recorded in Matthew 18. That is, dealing with disputes is central to the very definition of the church and indeed the presence of Christ's Spirit. In short, Paul addresses conflict in the church because he is a follower of Christ, a dedicated churchman. And to follow Christ, to be the church, means to reconcile the brother.

B. Conflict Ministries: The Center of Mission

If reconciliation is indeed central to God's intentions for salvation, and the church bears responsibility for the ministry of reconciliation, Christians need to reconsider the relationship between peacemaking and mission. The task is first of all to claim anew the vision of *shalom* God set before His creation. We must move ministries of peace from the periphery of Christian concern to the center where it belongs.

This means that when the church calls unbelievers to repentance, the call will be not merely to inner peace, but to reconciliation among humans. The church must take responsibility for inviting new believers, not merely to optional good works, but to participation in the concrete tasks of reconciliation, which are the primary manifestation of God's new creation.

Secondly, we must consider the connection between *what* we teach—the Gospel of peace—and *how* we teach. Missionaries observe that converts emphasize in their own faith activities in which the local missionaries spend the greatest amount of time.

Christ did not merely announce that the Good News is that the sick can be healed. He healed, and in the act proclaimed the kingdom. Word and deed are one, inseparable! Reconciliation is central to the Gospel and Christians must be active in reconciling to proclaim the Good News.

The Old Testament promises that in the act of ministry amidst conflict, God's children are themselves renewed. "If you take away...the yoke, the pointing of the finger..., if you pour yourself out for the hungry and satisfy the desire of the afflicted..., your ancient ruins shall be rebuilt..., you shall be called, the repairer of the breach, the restorer of paths to dwell in." (Isaiah 58:9-12.)

Conflict
Between
Groups

True peace is not merely the absence of tension, but it is the presence of justice and brotherhood.

—Martin Luther King

Third-party functions often useful in group conflicts include:
- *Humanizing the conflict.*
- *Establishing trust.*
- *Opening channels of communication.*
- *Supporting a flow of accurate information.*
- *Interpreting the issues.*
- *Furnishing pastoral support.*
- *Representing the concerns of the wider community.*
- *Advocating a non-violent but just and responsible resolution.*
- *Offering alternatives to repressive or violent strategies.*
- *Soliciting and providing resources.*
- *Observing all parties to the conflict.*
- *Testing and mobilizing support for proposals that may resolve conflict.*

—John Adams in "Ministries in Social Conflict"
Engage/Social Action Forum #43, pp. 17-24

Alternate channels of communication are desperately needed in the midst of a disagreement or conflict. Both groups may have persons skilled and equipped with all the technical tools of communicating. Yet, little information is being conveyed between the groups. The messages that are sent are often mistranslated even when they are in the same language. Consequently, at times when a great deal is at stake and when even simple signals cannot be sent between the groups, an alternate means of communication may be needed. When trusted persons or groups are near enough to the conflict they may find themselves serving that purpose—often within the full view of the opposing groups while their own communication equipment stands idle.

—Adams, **ibid.**

II / A Conceptual Framework

"Suppose a pastor... is willing to go and say: 'I am Mr. Smith of the Albright United Methodist Church and I want to express our concern for what is happening in our community and to see where we might be able to help.' With the contact a flow of information and insight begins that put the conflict into a new perspective."

"Presence is the first ministry to be considered in social conflict situations—getting next to and identifying with the problem. It is important not to identify prematurely with any one part of the conflict, since one of the purposes of a ministry of presence is to see every possible aspect of the conflict and to consider the full range of ministry that can be and may need to be performed.

A ministry of presence gives actual exposure to the many dimensions of the conflict. It allows for a much better understanding of what is taking place than would be obtained through newspaper reports, government releases, protest movement circulars, or the rumors that may be running through the community."

— John Adams in "Ministries in the Midst of Social Conflict,"
Engage/Social Action #43

I. Introduction

"For God so loved the world that he gave his only Son that whoever believes in him should not perish but have eternal life." (John 3:16)

"If a brother or sister is ill-clad and in lack of daily food, and one of you says to them, 'Go in peace, be warmed and filled' without giving them the things needed for the body, what does it profit?" (James 2:16, 17)

From a Christian perspective authentic peace requires both conversion and justice. The unique power of Christian faith and tradition lies in the fact that they speak directly to human relationships without being naive about the reality of personal wickedness. That is, Christianity at its best calls for justice and reconciliation, but also calls for a changed heart, a heart that is turned from self to God and to others. If Christians have failed in the calling of reconciliation, it is largely due to failure to balance these two perspectives.

The difficulty arises because the "peacemaker" never actually does what the title implies. No one can "make peace" for others. Christians point to a new reality, demonstrating its existence in word or deed in whatever way possible. But there is no assurance of success. Even where some semblance of justice can be achieved, one often knows that reconciliation can be only partial because the parties in a conflict do not share faith in the God of peace. Similarly, one frequently encounters situations where both parties claim personal faith in God, yet remain insensitive to issues of justice. The easiest response for the Christian peacemaker is to give up the task, or focus only on one dimension of it.

The challenge is to be present in conflict as a visible and audible testimony to a new reality without imposing Christian agenda on others or becoming discouraged when genuine peace is elusive.

Parties in conflict are faced with an array of options for resolution. Competition, coercion, retaliation, and violence are often the most attractive or popular choices. Amidst this array of destructive possibilities, the Christian peacemaker offers an alternative, a new method of relating to human conflict that also testifies to a new way of life.

The analogy of the seller of fine cheeses in a village market is perhaps useful here. The merchant knows his offerings are of superb quality. But how is he to convince others? He offers free samples of his wares—with no strings attached. Only then will people have the freedom to experience the truth for themselves.

In the same way, the Christian peacemaker goes about peacemaking in the world, knowing that manifesting the signs of God's reign is the best way to point to the reality of salvation. Here and there, the "seeds of peace" will fall, as in the Parable of the Sower, on fertile ground and others will come to know and love God.

II. Three Conditions For Peace

The doctor does not heal bodies but rather creates conditions under which healing can occur. Similarly, the Christian peacemaker does not "make peace," but rather helps to create those conditions which allow disputing parties to choose for peace and reconciliation.

Whether a dispute is inter-personal or inter-group in nature, the aims of the peacemaker are the same: to make peaceful settlement and cooperation a more attractive option for bringing change and resolving disagreement than coercion or violence; to attend to issues of justice; to stand with the disputing parties in working through their conflict; to enable parties to deal constructively with future conflicts.

In order to meet these aims, three conditions must be met:

A. **Atmosphere.** Disputing parties must be convinced that excessive competition, retaliation, coercion, foul play, and violence will be counter-productive for all, themselves included. A mutual problem-solving approach must be established as the best long-term method for serving one's own interests.

B. **Process Elements.** Elements necessary for carrying out a cooperative settlement process must be present:
1) Both parties must be able to articulate their concerns and sustain them in the face of opposition—otherwise the weak are simply crushed by the strong.
2) Relevant information must be available.
3) All potential resources for meeting the competing needs of parties must be explored.

C. **Forum.** A forum must exist enabling a cooperative settlement process to function.

Where these factors are met, reconciliation is in fact a likely possibility. The challenge for Christian peacemakers is thus: How can we help establish conditions necessary for peace?

III. Roles For Peacemakers

There are numerous roles open to the peacemaker committed to helping meet the conditions necessary for peace. Following chapters demonstrate use of these roles.

Roles Influencing Atmosphere

Proper attitudes and environment are essential for resolving conflict constructively. All disputes will be resolved sooner or later. The only question is **how** they will be resolved. How does a peacemaker enable parties to realize that they serve their own long-term interest by working nonviolently and cooperatively? The challenge is a tough one—probably the hardest part of conflict resolution. Chapter III recounts several incidents in which concerned groups took the role of **Observer** to help discourage violence. Establishing Observers is only one way of addressing the concern for proper atmosphere, and not a highly positive one at that. It commends itself mainly because it is readily established, has proven to be effective when other more positive methods are unworkable, and because it may lead to further positive roles by the Observers.

The roles of Sustainer or Legitimizer, discussed below, also help in creating proper atmosphere. If parties believe that others will help ensure that valid grievances will be aired, the disputants may be less prone to act violently or competitively in an effort to destroy the other party while the opportunity exists.

The mere willingness to meet with both parties and take seriously their grievances may also influence attitudes. The concern of an impartial third party helps convey to those in dispute that their opponents may not be quite so unreasonable or transparently wrong as they believe.

Finally, there is often a place for mere friendship for individuals in conflicts. Most of us have experienced the sense of alienation that often accompanies conflict—alienation not only from opponents, but from others, from all that is expansive and good; from God, the source of life. When people act destructively in conflicts, often it is because they are overwhelmed by a sense of alienation. Someone who knows how to be a genuine friend, who can listen and demonstrate caring can sometimes serve an important function in peacemaking by supporting individuals in fighting alienation.

Roles Effecting Process Elements

The first element essential to the functioning of a constructive conflict resolution process is the ability of both parties to make their complaints heard as relative equals. Weaker parties are always in danger of being crushed by the strong. When this happens, the symptoms of conflict may disappear, but the conflict remains. The weak suffer injustice. As soon as they have re-grouped, the conflict will emerge openly once again.

The "peacemaker" in this setting whose only goal is to "reduce conflict" is a pale and ineffective reconciler, and quite possibly a real liability to long-term justice and stability. Merely helping to vent emotions or create good feelings is not enough if basic inequities causing the hostility go unchanged. Rather than merely aiming to reduce conflict, the peacemaker must distinguish *constructive* from *destructive* conflict, and understand his or her goal as supporting constructive forms of conflict which can bring needed change.

Thus, paradoxically, the road to true peace sometimes lies through increased conflict. The peacemaker must help strenthen the position of the weaker party so that social change necessary for peace will occur. Conceptually, there are a number of roles in a conflict open to the peacemaker to meet this condition. They include Sustainer, Legitimizer, and Advocate.

The **Legitimizer** tries to help establish the credibility of the weaker party's needs in the eyes of the skeptical stronger party. The **Sustainer** goes a step further and locates resources enabling the weaker party to sustain their challenge: e.g, food, money, materials, public attention. The **Advocate** not only legitimizes and sustains the challenge of the weaker party, he also speaks openly with and on behalf of the weaker party, helping them to identify resources and articulate needs.

Finally, in order to make it possible for the two parties to make their complaints heard as relative equals, the peacemaker must avoid the temptation to undermine the efforts of activists already operating in a group conflict where power is unequal. Since activists are always busy rallying their forces and often speak in hostile tones, they may seem to some to be enemies of peace— they are feeding the dispute! The peacemaker understands, however, that where power is unequal the presence of activists is crucial to authentic peace, for the activist arouses energy which can be channeled toward constructive change.

The second element essential to the settlement process is accurate information. Parties in dispute tend to focus energy on posturing. A

Researcher can provide data that sometimes yields startling results.

The third element is resources adequate to satisfy the needs of both parties. Again, parties in conflict become preoccupied with defeating the other side rather than aiming to obtain resources that might allow all to win. The **Resource Expander** aids the resolution process by "adding a slice to the pie of conflict," marshalling all available resources so that everyone stands to win more.

Roles Creating A Forum

One veteran mediator defines dispute settlement as "exchanging promises about the future, in order to resolve a dispute now." The existence of a workable forum for channeling information and proposals—promises about the future—is crucial.

This forum can be either a person acting as **mediator** or an event which brings parties together in a **joint task** or discussion, or as a **mechanism** permanently available for resolving disputes.

Changing Roles

Ideally, the conflict intervenor can undertake several roles in a given conflict, either simultaneously or in sequence. This may not always be possible—to move from the role of Advocate to Mediator may prove unacceptable to one or both parties. In such cases the conflict intervenor must find others to fill the necessary role. The aim of the peacemaker is not to make the conflict resolution process dependent upon his or her own skills, but rather to ensure that conditions favorable for resolution are present.

The chapters that follow in the first section demonstrate these roles.

III / The Role of Observer

Establishing Observers is one way of addressing the concern for proper atmosphere. It commends itself mainly because it is readily established, has proven to be effective when other more positive methods are unworkable, and because it may lead to further positive roles by the Observers.
— From Chapter II

"We believed that by furnishing observers the religious community could help inhibit potentially violent types of protest, monitor the activities of the communications media, and help to avoid police overreaction as well as orienting a sizable and representative segment of the local community in a disciplined way."
— John Adams in **At the Heart of the Whirlwind**

Observers in a Farm Labor Dispute

Mix together United Farm Workers, Teamsters, unaffiliated workers, growers, vineyard foremen and sheriff's deputies and you have an explosive combination. In the summer of 1973 the Central Valley of California had been rocked by violent eruptions of that same mixture. But the next year a new ingredient was added when people of faith, clergy and laity alike, were present at points of possible confrontation. They were third-party observers, wearing orange vests emblazoned with the Spanish and English words "Observer/Observador." The bilingual two- and three-person teams stood apart from the adversaries with paper and pencils, ready to report each day's activities.

Since Cesar Chavez, Larry Itliong, and others began the organization of farm laborers in 1962, Delano and the surrounding areas of Kern and Tulare counties had been the center of the farm labor dispute. Without a farm labor law to channel the conflict through secret ballot representation, elections there had brought recurring violence in the fields and communities. With the new interest of the Teamsters' Union in the organization of the field workers, the summer of 1973 was particularly violent with many confrontations, numerous arrests, and one person killed on a picket line near Delano.

In an effort to avoid such violent repetitions, religious leaders formed the Inter-faith Committee of Concern, whose intent was: "to mobilize the good will of the community in declaring that while there may be conflict there must not be violence to persons or property." Observer teams were to be present at potentially abrasive locations in order to give "unbiased and objective reports of the events." This third party presence sought the endorsement and cooperation of all parties involved, who in turn would receive regular reports along with the general public and media.

The committee approached law enforcement agencies, including the sheriff, police, and district attorneys in each jurisdiction; the Teamsters' Union; growers through their various organizations; and the United Farm Worker's Union. Although sometimes wary of church involvement, all parties accepted the plan.

The response by people from the churches was mixed for the proposal seemed filled with many dangers. Not the least of these fears was the fear of actual physical danger for observers, and the fear of renewing the painful conflicts in the churches resulting from the long-term controversy. Most of the observers were drawn from the larger urban setting of Bakersfield, which was a little more insulated from the controversy. The community of Delano with its population of 15,000 yielded fewer participants because of the years of personal, painful conflict. Congregations were not asked to endorse the program officially but individuals were invited to volunteer. Before the summer ended over sixty people of Protestant, Catholic and Jewish faith had spent many, long hours in the hot sun together.

During July and August 1974, the Inter-faith Committee of Concern fielded two- and three-person observer teams for a month in the grape vineyards south of Bakersfield and for a month during the harvest in the two-county area around Delano. From the break of day through mid-afternoon, the teams followed picket parties from field to field, often forming processions with union and law enforcement vehicles. It was often hard even to find places from which to observe and not be identified with any of the parties.

All in all it was a non-violent season in the grape fields. Minor incidents of propoerty destruction and a brief period of "pushing and shoving" were the extent of the violence. There were no physical attacks upon persons observed. The many sharp verbal exchanges that might have escalated into physical violence were "cooled" by the self-restraint of one party or another.

Media representatives and community leaders credited the observer teams with keeping the conflict in the fields minimal. The members of the committee credited the participants with self-restraint.

Reports of the committee were reprinted almost verbatim in the local newspaper. These reports discouraged gossip and rumor by providing accurate reports of activities in the fields. —**John M. Foster, pastor, First United Methodist Church, Delano, California.**

Religious Observers at Miami Beach

In 1971, the news came to Miami Beach that both Republican and Democrat national conventions would be held in their city in 1972. The announcement brought considerable concern to many individuals in Miami Beach. Everyone remembered vividly the violence of the 1968 Democratic national convention in Chicago.

As early as July, 1971, leaders in the religious community of Miami began to plan for the upcoming political conventions. Perhaps, with adequate preparation, the churches could play a role in preventing violence. A group of 'Protestant leaders called national and local religious leaders to a meeting. They hoped to create a plan by which church agencies could work toward maintaining peace and stability in the community during the convention while at the same time supporting citizens and organized groups exercising their rights of freedom of speech and assembly. Sixteen local religious representatives gathered at that meeting and formed an organization named "Religious and Community Leaders Concerned." Then followed many months of preparation for the conventions.

In March, RCLC sponsored an "Awareness Seminar" to prepare the community for the conventions. Local police officials were invited and asked to address the meeting. The manager of the Democratic Convention was asked to participate. This Awareness Seminar was intended to "legitimize" the work of RCLC in the eyes of the "establishment." At about the same time, RCLC representatives began contacting leaders of the various movement groups intending to come to the Democratic National Convention. These groups included the Southern Christian Leadership Conference, the National Welfare Rights Organization, the National Tenants' Organization and the United Farm Workers Organization.

John Adams, in his book, *At the Heart of the Whirlwind*, summarizes the concerns of RCLC during this period as follows:
1) Orienting the general public toward citizen involvement in support for the conventions. Besides the awareness seminar, several other initiatives were taken to build a stable base of support from the community.
2) Opening lines of communication with prospective protest groups, law enforcement agencies, government offices and political parties.
3) Seeking legitimation of RCLC involvement from all parts of the local religious community and also from national religious groups.

With these contacts established, RCLC began planning for widespread presence of "observers." Plans were made for locating these volunteers at various strategic spots in and around the convention center. The largest number of observers would be spotted on the streets and at hotel headquarters of the political parties and the various candidates. More than 300 persons were recruited from churches and synagogues of the Greater Miami area for this role. Adams notes that these plans for "observing" were seriously questioned by many groups. "The 'movement' representatives wanted to know for whom RCLC would be observing and just what would be done with the information it obtained. Some police representatives were cool toward having RCLC closely observe and record police actions on the streets. Many members in the religious community itself thought that 'observing' was far too neutral a role for the religious community to play in such a potentially violent situation. Other people felt that the religious community should be an issue-advocate, marching with the protesters. Some believed that churches and synagogues should primarily support the police to protect the community rather than protest with the dissenters."

"We believed that by furnishing observers the religious community could help inhibit potentially violent types of protest, monitor the activities of the communications media, and help to avoid police overreaction as well as orient a sizable and representative segment of the local community in a disciplined way."

"All observers trained for twelve hours and took part in exercises which equipped them to observe as impartially, objectively, accurately, and as rapidly as possible. Movement representatives and personnel from the Miami Beach police department participated in the training."

An operation center was set up to which the observers reported for their shifts and to which they later reported by telephone to a special communication center manned by RCLC volunteer operators. A daily composite report was made between 4 a.m. and 8 a.m., and one copy of this report was promptly delivered to each of the movement groups, the chief of police, the Community Relations Service of the U.S. Department of Justice, and to the Convention Ushering Service.

The composite report served several functions. For one, it served as an additional "truth bearer" or "reality-tester", as some individuals termed it. For another, it demonstrated that the observers were filling a special role and were not mere bystanders or curiosity seekers. Perhaps most important, the composite reports showed that observers did not single out any segment of the convention scene for special scrutiny.

RCLC also ended up in other roles. Perhaps one of the most important was helping to maintain peaceful interaction between officials and various protest groups encamped at various sites throughout Miami Beach. RCLC assisted in obtaining camping permits from the city council and then worked as a coordinator with the groups in maintaining communication with the city and among each other. When the disruptive behavior of one small group, the Zippies, threatened the withdrawal of camping privileges from all groups, RCLC called a meeting with representatives from the various groups, and succeeded in gaining cooperation.

On a few occasions police undertook action that seemed calculated to create confrontation. At one point, 30 Miami police entered the campsite of demonstrators shortly after midnight and, with no provocation, proceeded to chase young people. Police cars and motorcycles began closely circling the park. Tension mounted. The campers began arming themselves with rocks, sticks, and other make-shift weapons. John Adams called the police command post and requested removal of the police from the area, at least temporarily. He was told that no police were authorized to be in the area. Adams then requested that barricades be placed at intersections surrounding the park in order to stop the flow of traffic, including the unauthorized patrol cars. Within ten minutes, Miami Beach scout cars arrived, the streets were closed to traffic, and the confrontation ceased.

In the end, the religious community was credited by all sides for a significant role. The protest groups, the police, the community, and one segment of the democratic process had been safeguarded from destruction and chaos.

Adams summarizes his own understanding of the experience as follows: "During the 1972 political conventions the religious community learned that it does not always have to be an activist or an advocate in crisis situations. Sometimes all that is required is to be present and to be identified as 'impartial observers' to prevent useless confrontations."

"When planning begins early enough, when lines of communication are adequately opened, and when the rights of all persons are given sufficient consideration both by those in power and those challenging public policy, there can be peaceful and effective protest." *

Training Observers for Kent State University

An Observer Team composed of faculty and staff members was formed at Kent State University to serve on the occasion of the first anniversary observances of the May 1970 killings. Two workshops of two hours each were conducted by Charles Walker, of the Haverford Center for Nonviolent Conflict Resolution. What follows is the outline of subject matter covered in the workshop. (The administration had set up a Communications Center for the time covering the special events.) This outline was also used in a 1976 project in Capetown, South Africa, and in 1978 when squatter camps were scheduled for demolition. Reprinted with permission of Charles Walker and the Gandhi Institute, Box 92, Cheyney, Pa.

A. Mandate

1. **To whom responsible?** Faculty, administration, trustees, students, public? Conclusion: the civil peace of Kent State and those whom that civil peace embraces.

---

*Information and quotes from *At the Heart of the Whirlwind* by John P. Adams, (Harper & Row, 1976), pp. 86-99.

2. **To whom report?** Conclusion:
   - anyone who wants to know; information is available
   - anyone who needs to know; take the initiative to get the information to those who need it.

B. Let the Existence of the Team Be Known

1. Write up a **statement of purpose**: what you intend to do and how you intend to do it. Keep it concise.

2. **Publish statement** in the school paper, either as a news story or a letter to the editor.

3. **Talk with key people in advance**, personally and not only in groups.

4. **Attend meetings of groups about the anniversary events to gain visibility**: get introduced, explain purpose and function.

5. Have **armbands or sign of identification** on hand, if and when needed. Seems as if high visibility is called for during events, perhaps also when attending certain meetings.

C. Communication During Operations

1. **Patrols (teams) report in** periodically. One at Observers Center travels around occasionally to get or supplement reports.

2. **Walkie-talkies** to Observers Center and/or Communications Center. Keep their use minimal and as unobtrusive as possible without concealing them.

3. **Coordinator** or coordinating team member may go to anyone as needed, e.g. head of security.

4. Work in **teams of two or three. Stay together** and keep each other up to date. Evaluate information as it comes in.

5. **Locate phones** around campus, pay phones, too; perhaps arrange to have key to an office for emergency calls.

D. Recording Information

1. **Notebooks**: for names, times, rumors, brief notes. Don't be too cryptic, or so hasty as to write undecipherable notes.

2. **Pocket tape recorders** are very useful to get longer field notes recorded; need not transcribe, but will be a reminder.

3. Hold **team meetings**, perhaps at breakfast time and/or in the evening, to:
   a. evaluate information
   b. discuss key incidents
   c. work out assignments
   d. clarify or modify procedures

4. Develop a **transcript** (each day if possible) which the team agrees upon. Then dispose of raw notes, which may be misinterpreted or misused if subpoened, or stolen.

E. Transmitting Information

1. To **Communications Center**: walkie-talkie, phone, in person, by messenger. Receiver at Center should write in a log the informant, the message, to whom the message goes, and the time. Same for Observers Center if at a different place.

2. To student and other **activity centers**.

3. To school **paper** and school **radio**.

4. At times to **reporters**. *Be careful,* do this only when it appears absolutely necessary to correct false statements, impressions or rumors. Perhaps two members of the Team should agree on anything given to reporters in this circumstance.

F. Getting Ready

1. Prepare **list of all observers**: name, department, formal title, phone number at office and home.

2. Work out **assignments**, in teams as much as possible. Keep a good spirit in giving and receiving instructions or counsel.

3. **Attend:**
   a. training sessions, briefing sessions
   b. preliminary rallies
   c. press conferences
   d. planning meetings

4. **Study:**
   a. staging: geography, promontories, routes of march, etc.
   b. parties involved: demonstrators, bystanders, press, police, security guards, officials (school, governmental).

5. **Test communications systems** to the extent practicable.

G. In Action

Note: most of the skills are simply those of a good reporter, though employed less obtrusively; for example:

1. **Avoid partisan actions**, hostile questions, rhetorical questions.

2. **Keep demeanor** in accord with role.

3. Write down—don't try to remember—relevant information, names, times when something happens. Be sure spelling is accurate.

4. **Seek out high ground** so as to be able to see what happens. At a meeting, stay near or on stage, or speakers' stand.

5. **Avoid concealing your role.** There may be times when it is best not to advertise it, but it's hard to envisage an occasion when it should be concealed. The existence of the Observer Team is a statement of intent, about helping to avoid or forestall violence and disorder.

6. **Follow arrested or detained group** to jail or magistrate's court. *Careful observing and reporting of these situations is crucial, for they are often the source of many rumors.* Get names, addresses, phone numbers, charges, status of case, hearing date and time. Perhaps be helpful within role, e.g. get word to someone whom an arrested person wants to notify. Go in your own car, not in one belonging to someone else, so as to maintain freedom of movement.

7. At a scene of violence or disorder, **do not usurp role of police or security people,** or interfere (see next section) with ensuing actions. The Observer Team and the press are on equal ground, but the observers will be watching the press too. Don't get so absorbed in the action that words spoken or shouted are not understood accurately. Difficult as it may be, try to record accurately and as fully as possible who said what. Even the time may become important if litigation results.

H. Change Role?

Times may come when an observer feels impelled to change role, e.g. to become a demonstrator, if one thing leads to another, or something outrageous happens to prompt an observer to intervene. In this event:

1. Make a decision—then live with it; don't apologize or over-explain.

2. Take off observer identification at once.

3. Notify fellow team member—it will probably be a sudden decision—who should notify coordinator of Observer Team as soon as possible.

4. After the decision, other observers should accept it without getting uptight—won't do any good anyway. Others in the team need to take up the slack.

5. **Record this incident in detail.**

I. General Notes

1. Use teams system at all possible points if you have enough people available: at Team Center, on patrols, field groups, when speaking on behalf of the group. Working in teams pays high dividends in difficult and unpredictable situations.

2. There needs to be a Team Center inside (where coffee, paper, notebooks, etc., are available) and an outside Field Center for reporting in, monitoring operations, deciding ad hoc matters, or suddenly deploying teams or individuals. One need may be a "runner" who won't object to running errands, getting materials or bearing messages; at the Field Center, at the Team Center. There should be a phone at the Team Center.

3. In the midst of protracted observations, e.g, an event lasting four hours, hold a Team meeting to check out what is happening and whether the Team is functioning well. Over multi-day happenings, Team should meet twice daily. Confine purely organizational matters to one of the meetings. Post notice of any meeting time changes.

4. Try to keep ahead of the action. After a planning session, seek out responsible spokespersons to find out schedules, coming events, names of speakers and chairpersons, route of march, etc. **Arrive well in advance of scheduled time**, observe the staging, initiation and unfolding of the event.

5. Keep oral reports concise without leaving out important parts. Here is a weak point in many operations; reporters may exaggerate (betrayed by feeling of self-importance) may not be accurate or fail to check out details. Reporting sessions can get too long. Leave time to select and write out the parts of each oral report which should be included in the final report.

6. Appoint a historian of the project, or get a researcher to perform this function. Collect all duplicated material that is passed out, put date on it (time if important)—all items produced by the Observer Team, except raw notes. Note suggestion of log at Observer Team and Communication Centers. The workings and results of the Observer Team may have a variety of uses, some of them unforeseen. One is to help other such endeavors.

J. Final Report

1. As end of project nears, designate a person or team to prepare an outline for a final report. Get critiques. Assemble material already drafted. Prepare distribution list.

2. Prepare first draft, duplicate several copies. Include a chronology of major events.

3. Show to major parties and invite comments, corrections. Look for important omissions.

4. Complete final draft, duplicate. Don't fail to put date on it!

5. Present to all major parties, others on distribution list.

6. Hold a reserve supply for anyone who asks, consistent with distribution budget, and for unforeseen uses later. When preparing the project budget, put in a substantial item for duplicating and distributing the report.

7. Arrange to discuss the report with key people. Be careful to distinguish what is a personal view or interpretation from the consensus represented by the report.

8. Decide on spokespersons for Observer Team in case need arises: press conference, litigation, writers, researchers, involved persons.

IV / The Role of Legitimizer

In the pre-dawn darkness of May 14, 1974, a group of Mohawk Indians moved into Moss Lake, an abandoned Girl Scout camp in northern New York. Most of the group came from the Akwesasne reservation, which straddles the border between New York and Canada.

They had come, they soon made clear to the world around, to re-claim part of the Mohawk ancestral homeland. The Mohawks have long contested the legality of a treaty giving their land to the State of New York in the 18th century, saying that one person had without authorization signed away all his people's land.

They had also come with the intent to live the native way of life, undisturbed by white people. One of them said to an observer, "Your government lets the Amish live the way they want to; why can't they let us live the way we want to?" They brought some farm animals and made plans to grow their own garden supplies.

Not surprisingly, the surrounding community did not appreciate the intentions of the Mohawks. Many local whites were hostile and vigilantes took to roaring past in cars, sending rifle shots over the camp. State troopers were sent in, who held the camp under surveillance, and posted armed guards. A state senator accused the group of being "radical."

The Mohawks needed food and supplies. Local Mennonites responded by donating pick-up loads of supplies—vegetables, sweet corn, carrots, potatoes, onions, warm clothing and live hens. After a visit by MCC staffer Paul Leatherman, and a local Mennonite bishop, Richard Zehr, MCC sent canned meat, potatoes, and flour; and assisted in securing farm implements. Zehr and his family visited the camp on numerous occasions and developed friendship with the Mohawks.

With the help of a mediator, negotiations were eventually set up and steady progress was made. Over a period of many months, a peaceful settlement satisfactory to all parties was carefully worked out. The State and the Mohawks agreed to a new site in Clinton County, New York. The Indians received 700 acres of lakes and woodland, plus irrevocable fishing and hunting rights on 5,000 acres of additional lands. The dispute officially ended May 14, 1977, exactly three years after the original take-over of land, with the signing of the agreement.

The move from Moss Lake to the new site was a major task. MCC and local Mennonite churches joined with other church groups in helping to pay expenses for gas and truck rental. At "Ganienkeh," as they christened their new home, the Mohawks built a home for each family and erected a building for common use from used lumber. From a donation, they purchased a used sawmill, to furnish their own lumber and provide income. They also bought a small stone-crusher. With the support of agricultural agents from Cornell University, they began laying out fields and raising crops.

In retrospect, the role of the local Mennonite congregations was a significant peacemaking effort for several reasons. For one, it *sustained* the Indians, physically, and morally, enabling them to make their complaints heard without being immediately silenced by their opposition. In such an event, symptoms may have ended, but not the conflict. Equally important, the congregations communicated both to the Indians and to the white community that the way of Christ is one of good will and generosity, not hatred and selfishness. Observers credit the churches for being a significant factor in reversing hostility in the community. Officials took the Indians with greater seriousness as it became clear that some people cared about the outcome of the conflict. And those hostile locally were eventually outweighed by the good-will acts of the churches.

Today several dozen families live at Ganienkeh. Commented Zehr after a visit in October, 1978, "They are fast becoming self-sustaining, which was their goal from the beginning." The Mohawks expressed their goals in a written statement of purpose published after their arrival at Ganienkeh. Their aim—"To build a nation of peace that knows no hatred for any man; to be self-sufficient and ask no one to bear another's burden; to use nature's gifts with care and respect; to live by the laws of nature."

V / The Role of Advocate

Advocacy is sometimes an essential tool for resolving conflicts. Frequently one party in a dispute does not possess the resources for pursuing peaceful and constructive solutions to conflict. In such a situation the intervenor works actively on behalf of the weaker party or arranges for another third-party to do so, helping to follow through with peaceful strategies. Advocacy may at first sharpen the conflict, but in the long run, it is the only way to peace in some conflicts. If one party is unable for lack of resources or organizational skill to pursue just claims, the dispute will fester even if open conflict has disappeared. Eventaully, a small event may trigger an explosive flare-up.

Advocacy raises ethical and, for some Christians, theological questions. How far will the Christian intervenor go in the role of advocate? What if the intervenor disagrees with some values of the party being advocated?

But advocacy itself is not a new or unusual role for Christians. To take an example from my own Christian heritage, history shows Mennonites to be skillful, if somewhat uncomfortable, in advocacy. Mennonites have successfully taken an advocate role in relation to governments (e.g.: conscription), schools, and other institutions, on behalf of their own interests.

The most recent example of such advocacy is the well-publicized intervention of Canadian and U.S. Mennonites on behalf of the Old Colony Mennonites in Seminole, Texas, 1977 to 1980. Official Mennonite bodies in both Canada and the U.S. sent several intervenors to Texas in the role of Fact-finder, or Researcher, with the expectation that reports from these intervenors would support the claims of the Old Colony Mennonites who had moved from Mexico and requested resident status in the U.S. Numerous Mennonites also journeyed to Washington, D.C. to meet with legislators and immigration authorities. When special legislation was introduced in Congress, on behalf of the 620 Old Colony members, many Mennonites wrote letters to Congress to urge support for these victims of dishonesty and misinformation.

The question thus is not "Can we be advocates?" but "How will we advocate?" and "On whose behalf?" There are many ways to advocate in addition to the abrasive Alinsky-style tactics that many have associated with the role in the past two decades. Seeking God's will in the midst of injustice Christians will always struggle with the question of "how?" The answers must come in concrete ministry and prayer. But let us at least commit ourselves to extending those forms of advocacy we are willing and able to use for our own benefit to support the poor, the captives, and the hungry.

The following two narratives exemplify two kinds of advocacy roles. The first story was told by Hubert Schwartzentruber about Macler Shepherd, a black Mennonite who led a community revival in a severely depressed area of St. Louis,

*Missouri. Shepherd's involvement is an example of short-term crisis advocacy.
Shepherd responded to the needs of the situation, used his influence and
knowledge of the community to avert a violent confrontation and moved on.*

*The second story is an example of strategic, long-term advocacy. At requests
from local members, the United Churches of Christ took a strong advocate stance
on behalf of the black community in Wilmington, North Carolina. Although the
church's role was not always a popular one, it has been effective. Due to the
widespread attention given to the situation, individuals imprisoned for racial
justice activities have been freed, and the "Wilmington Ten" case has been
removed from the "political oppression" rosters of the well-reputed Amnesty
International. In December 1980, charges against the "Wilmington Ten" were
overturned by a federal appeals panel.*

*Advocacy is the most demanding activity for peacemakers, the role perhaps
least assured of success, the most prone to being misunderstood. But then, should
followers of the crucified Christ expect otherwise?*

Youth and Police in St. Louis

"I recall at one point a near riot was in the making several blocks from
Macler's shop. The incident was around a confrontation of the police and
some youth who were being apprehended for apparently no good reason.
The youth resisted arrest and additional police were called in for more
reinforcement. Immediately approximately 25 police cars appeared.
Macler saw the event happening and proceeded to intervene. Macler did
not take a neutral position but took a pro-youth position. He immediately
asked the police to postpone arresting the youth until some black
policemen were present. The police responded. The youth were fearful of
being beaten immediately when they were delivered to the police station.
That was a procedure often used by St. Louis police. Macler was able to
assure the youth that they would not be beaten. At that point already 500
or more neighborhood people had gathered with bricks, bottles, and other
objects to begin the confrontation. A police car was overthrown. In that
incident Macler was able to cool tempers enough so that the youth could be
taken to the police station; the crowd finally did disappear, and the youth
were not booked for any offense. Had Macler not arrived at precisely that
moment, a full-scale riot would have taken place in the next 20 minutes.
Macler, however, did not take a neutral position. He very clearly and firmly
confronted the police and their policy. He made his support for the youth
who committed no offense very clear. The result was that no riot occurred. I
could cite at least two or three other such incidents where Macler was able
to intervene. The only way that Macler could intervene was because of his
understanding of the community and being known by the community,
both the residents and the establishment, and his own personal concern
for the welfare of human beings. While every major city in the U.S. had riots
during the 60's, there was not one incident of any rioting or even brush
fires in St. Louis. My judgment on that is that St. Louis had a Macler
Shepard who was able to effect authentic conciliation."

34

The Church and the Wilmington Ten*

In February 1971 in Wilmington, North Carolina, tensions resulting from desegregation of the city's public schools culminated in several days and nights of unrest in Wilmington, including two deaths and the burning of a grocery store. Nearly a year later charges were brought against 16 persons (later reduced to 10) for burning down the grocery store, whereupon they were jailed for four months without bail. The "Wilmington 10," as they came to be known—nine black males and one white female—were tried, found guilty, and sentenced to a combined total of 282 years in prison. Despite numerous appeals, they all returned to prison in February 1976 to begin serving their sentences. Except for the white woman who had the lightest sentence and was released on parole in the spring of 1977, all are in prison.

For me, the Wilmington 10 case might have remained simply a story, another instance of injustice, had not one of the defendants entered Talladega College in Alabama where I teach. Following the trial William "Joe" Wright was out on bail and became first my student, then my friend. Gradually I became more and more involved with both him and the case, assisting with personal matters, relaying messages, even assisting with aspects of his case. And as I learned to know Joe, I began to understand the tremendous burden, and the scars, which this case has placed upon him. He is now in prison—and has been in prison longer than even I with my skepticism about justice in this land expected him to be. The license plates of the state that has imprisoned him, incidentally, declare that North Carolina is "First in Freedom."

The story began in Wilmington, an economically insecure port city (in the southeastern part of North Carolina) with a long history of racial tensions. In the fall of 1970, court-ordered school desegregation took place. Black high schools with long and often proud traditions were demoted to junior high schools, with students and faculty getting distributed among the previously all-white schools. Many students were now in a minority situation for the first time.

Demands for increased black participation in school affairs began, culminating in a demonstration in January 1971 when one high school refused to allow an assembly program to be dedicated to the honor of Martin Luther King, Jr. Student leaders were expelled, and some violence occurred—perpetuated, it appears, mainly by whites.

Students then decided on a boycott, and the local United Church of Christ opened its doors to boycotting students and community persons. Community support grew, but so did tensions, and the local U.C.C. minister finally appealed to the main church offices for leadership. The Commission for Racial Justice of the U.C.C. then sent Rev. Ben Chavis, an experienced community activist and mediator, to Wilmington, to assist.

*By Howard Zehr, Jr. Reprinted from *Gospel Herald*. Nov. 1, 1977. Portions deleted.

A massive protest was organized to which the white community reacted with violence. The church asked for a curfew, but the city refused to respond. There followed several nights of near-guerilla warfare, with whites driving through black neighborhoods and shooting at unarmed blacks. The Ku Klux Klan and its more extreme relative, the Rights of White People (ROWP), roamed streets in what amounted to an armed siege of the black community. Some reports indicate that a few of the blacks who had barricaded themselves in churches and houses fired back. Two lives were lost and thousands of dollars' worth of property was damaged.

Almost a year later, warrants were issued for the arrest of 16 persons. This was later reduced to 10, including one white woman (an antipoverty worker), and nine black men (Ben Chavis and eight high school students). They were charged with arson and conspiracy in connection with the burning of one building, Mike's Grocery (no charges were ever brought for the deaths of the two victims). Bails were set high and the accused spent about four months in jail before their case came to trial in June 1972.

The trial seemed strange in many ways, even at the time. When a jury was selected which consisted of 10 blacks and two whites, the prosecutor became mysteriously ill, resulting in a postponement. When a new jury was drawn, it was 10 whites and two elderly blacks. The key witness for the state was a young man with a criminal record and a history of mental illness. Several key witnesses for the defense were threatened and failed to turn up in court. Consequently, the 10 were quickly found guilty and sentenced to incredibly severe prison sentences, averaging 28 years, with Ben Chavis drawing the heaviest sentence of 34 years. The combined total of the sentences came to 282 years for the alleged burning of one store. Appeal bail was set high— a total of over $400,000— but this was met by the United Church of Christ which has provided the primary financial support for the case.

Since the trial, the Wilmington 10 case has gone through a complex labyrinth of appeals, hearings, and motions. The irregularities multiply, yet the 10 still have not received a new trial. A recent post-conviction hearing is a case in point.

At the hearing, which lasted two weeks in the summer of 1977, evidence was presented to show that the three major prosecution witnesses have admitted to lying in the original trial and, in fact, claim to have been coached and even bribed for their testimony. Defense witnesses have now come forward, providing evidence that none of the 10 was at the scene of the crime. One state witness has even admitted to setting fire to the grocery, the crime for which the 10 are charged. Important evidence has been shown to have been kept from the defense in the original trial. And there is more, which would require too much space to delineate.

Yet the judge at the hearing, taking an extremely narrow view of his duty in this case, ruled that no constitutional rights had been violated. Therefore, he said, no new trial should be held— refusing to concern himself with whether or not justice had been done in the original trial.

It is an extraordinary case, and one can only conclude that these nine*
young men and one woman were and are being tried for political reasons.
Amnesty International in fact, has included the Wilmington 10 in their
catalog of worldwide political prisoners. Only by looking at the case in
terms of underlying political-racial factors can one start to explain why the
state sought and obtained such severe sentences, why it has persisted so
strenuously in denying a new trial, and why it has gone to such lengths to
see that the 10 are kept in prison.

Ben Chavis, it is generally felt, was and is a primary target. Chavis, a mild-
mannered but extremely dedicated and effective minister, had been
involved in the struggle for justice before. The state appeared determined
to silence effective black leadership and it is believed they particularly
wanted Ben Chavis. But the imprisonment of the Wilmington 10 also
seemed to be an effort to put down black attempts at change generally.

America claims to have no political criminals. In fact, unlike many other
Western nations, we have no official category known as "political crimes."
Perhaps the Wilmington 10 case, along with a series of others in U.S.
history, will help put that myth to rest.

Ironically, almost all of those involved in this trial, regardless of whose
side they are on, have in some way become victims. Everyone has suffered:
10 young people have had their lives permanently altered by the experience
of court and prison. Witnesses for the state and the defense have suffered,
too—often at the hands of the state— but harassment has come from
persons with loyalties on both sides.

In my view, the Wilmington 10 case is not merely an aberration in our
system of law, a simple miscarriage of justice. Rather, I believe it is a sign
that the system itself is not working right, that it can be used to repress
those who are poor and who challenge the system. If the Wilmington 10
conviction sticks, then we are all victims.

VI / The Role of Resources Expander

"Parties in conflict become preoccupied with defeating the other side rather than aiming to obtain resources that might allow all to win. The Resources Expander aids the resolution process by 'adding a slice to the pie of conflict,' marshalling all available resources so that everyone stands to win more."
— Chapter II

"The church has some unique resources for ministering in social conflicts. It has buildings and equipment near to almost any domestic conflict. It has a large group of prospective volunteers with a variety of skills. It maintains a communications network that is unmatched. It has a regular educational program to reach its own constituency. It has contacts across the community and probably has members within any of the groups that may be parties to the conflicts. It has the capacity for quickly mobilizing resources and raising support funds."
— John Adams in "Ministries in the Midst of Social Conflict,"
Engage/Social Action #43

In the early 1970's a large low-income housing development was constructed in New York City's Lower East Side. As the development neared completion, a bitter dispute divided the community: Who would be allowed to occupy the units?

The New York City Housing Authority had decided to lease some apartments in the unfinished 360-unit development to residents of the area around the site. Most of these residents were elderly orthodox Jews. But this decision contravened the Authority's policy of giving top priority to former-site occupants, most of whom were Hispanics.* The Puerto Rican neighborhood coalition sued the Housing Authority, along with the Federal Department of Housing and Urban Development. For more than two years the issue was contested in the courts. All the while, the apartments remained vacant.

Both sides recognized that it would be difficult for the courts to resolve the central issue—the racial and ethnic balance of the new housing complex and the Seward Park community—and the courts themselves had

*The following text is reprinted with permission from *Mediating Social Conflict* (Ford Foundation, 1978), pp. 13-15.

38

no appetite for a definitive ruling. Puerto Rican leaders feared that many of the residents would leave the area before the dispute was finally settled. The representatives of the Jewish community were concerned about the safety of their elderly constituents, not to mention their life expectancy. "We were concerned that many of the elderly would have died before this was resolved in the courts," says Kalman Finkel, the Legal Aid attorney who intervened on behalf of the Jewish residents. There was also a concern about crime and violence in the area surrounding the development. Getting into the project, they felt, was a matter of protecting their lives. Also, Finkel points out, "No politician in this city wanted to touch the dispute. However it was settled, a politician figured he had to lose something in a fight between Puerto Ricans and Jews."

George Nicolau of the Institute of Mediation and Conflict Resolution was approached to intervene in the dispute. To achieve a settlement, Nicolau had to meet three challenges: to win the trust of both sides, to dissipate the anger and focus the disputants on the real issues, and to devise a settlement that would provide public-housing apartments to both sides in sufficient number to satisfy the disputants.

Both sides were wary and on the lookout for any signs of favoritism by the mediator. Having been director of the antipoverty program in New York, Nicolau knew the attorney who represented the Hispanic coalition, but was not familiar with the other side; this created suspicion which Nicolau had to overcome by open-handed dealing with both sides.

For three months Nicolau met separately with the two groups, hoping to prepare each to understand the intricacies of the situation. "I wanted them to start thinking about hard realities, not the ideal solution," he says.

When he judged the time was right, Nicolau told one group he thought the other side was prepared to make an offer. However, he advised them not to accept or reject the offer immediately but to ask questions and get complete details of what the other side was offering. Discussion led to clarification of the situation. "They found out they were talking about a lot less people than they thought," Nicolau recalls. "Some people had left the neighborhood. In some cases the number of rooms in the available apartments didn't meet their needs. Some of the people wanted only ground-floor apartments. For the first time we had a realistic sense of what was involved."

Finkel believes that Nicolau's approach helped dissolve tension: "We started talking numbers, not principles. He made the representatives of each group responsible for talking reason and facts to their constituents."

Nicolau's familiarity with the political structure and government bureaucracy in New York and his association with community leaders and religious and racial spokesmen were vital factors in his mediation efforts. He skillfully involved the power brokers in the settlement, thus securing the resources that made an agreement possible.

When he had an accurate estimate of the number of people from both groups seeking apartments in the Seward Park project, he entered into discussions with the Grand Street Guild, a housing corporation of St. Mary's Church, which was then constructing a housing development alongside Seward Park. The Roman Catholic Archdiocese of New York agreed to provide 160 still unrented low-income apartments in this development to both Hispanics and orthodox Jews who had wanted to rent apartments in the Seward Park project. Nicolau then negotiated an agreement with the city housing authority to make apartments available in other desirable city projects to families who could not be accommodated in either the Guild or the Seward Park project. With tensions lowered and the parties indicating a willingness to consider some form of compromise, Nicolau was able to announce additional units were now available, and an agreement followed relatively quickly.

The resolution did not end Nicolau's involvement. District Court Judge Morris E. Lasker in February, 1974, five months after mediation began, asked Nicolau and a housing authority official to monitor the renting of the Seward Park apartments so that the agreed-upon formula of 60% non-white and 40% white was maintained.

VII / The Role of Mediator

Mediating A Racial Dispute

Beacon is a town of 14,000 in southeastern New York State. Every year Beacon has a town carnival. And every year, as well, beginning back in the 1960's, Beacon has experienced racial confrontations at the end of the carnival. Typically, the incidents consisted of a few isolated skirmishes between black and white youth.

In the summer of 1977, however, the skirmishes escalated to riot proportions. Bottles, knives and handguns appeared as weapons. For several evenings, carloads of youth—white, black, and brown—rocketed through the town. Brawls raged. Intoxicated with violence, the rioters turned in a frenzy to destroying downtown stores. Windows were smashed and widespread looting took place.

In the aftermath of the riot, the Beacon Chamber of Commerce asked assistance from the Community Relations Service, an agency of the Justice Department, to improve race relations in Beacon. Victor Risso, a Hispanic mediator was assigned to the situation.

Risso's initial strategy was simply to "talk with anyone who'd talk." His discussions quickly identified a wide range of difficulties in Beacon. The town was rent by factionalism— not only between the black, white and emerging brown communities, but also *within* these communities. The white Police Chief was notoriously racist and intransigent. The local community center was in a black neighborhood and viewed as strictly black "turf."

The mayor refused to take action on racial matters, insisting he was powerless to improve race relations. The NAACP and local churches had in the past attempted to initiate discussion following previous racial confrontations. Thus, when Risso broached the possibility of convening a discussion/planning group, initial response was negative. "We've already tried that and it doesn't work," came the reply. Risso soon found out, however, that previous discussions had ended after one or two sessions. He was determined to persevere beyond token gestures.

Since the Chamber of Commerce seemed to have good relationships in the community, Risso requested their assistance in convening a meeting with 40 representatives of the white, black, and brown populations, including the various factions within each group; as well as community service agencies, churches, the NAACP, and the city Recreation Department. The Chamber of Commerce called each individual several times to ensure good attendance.

"Groups came together in that meeting who had never communicated before," Risso recalls. Much of the meeting was spent in "ventilation," spilling out the emotions of the street by one group after another. But the group was able to agree on one thing, and that proved to be enough. They would continue holding regular discussion sessions.

At least once monthly, sometimes more often, the group met to discuss the situation in Beacon. In all, between 15 and 20 meetings were held. Participation was transitory, but gradually a nucleus emerged. In order to encourage attendance, minutes of meetings were sent only to participants.

At the third meeting a second significant agreement came. Participants agreed to form a community alliance, which they promptly dubbed S.O.B.— Spirit of Beacon.

In the long sequence of meetings that followed, the S.O.B. was rewarded for their perseverance. The County Recreation Department agreed to plan more activities for youth. A local corporation, IBM, granted $1,500 to support the S.O.B. The city Human Rights Commission, once virtually defunct, was revived and began acting aggressively on civil rights issues. The Police Chief, a white racist in the eyes of many, was replaced with a black chief.

Perhaps even more important, the planning meetings became occasion for airing grievances and establishing trust among the many community factions. The black community, for example, experienced a new sense of unity after unprecedented discussion between a radical black Islamic sect active in the city and traditionally-oriented black leaders.

The culmination of many months of discussions came on S.O.B. Day, a city-wide cultural festival celebrating the diverse cultures of the city. Ethnic food and music, friendly competition in children's skateboard and bicycle contests, and a holiday atmosphere aroused the enthusiastic participation of a broad spectrum of citizens. The day ended with no incidents of violence.

Risso, the Hispanic mediator who served as catalyst for these activities, does not claim to have resolved any particular disputes. "We simply established dialogue," he notes. In this case establishing dialogue seems to have been enough. Planning is currently underway for the fourth annual S.O.B. Day. From all indications the next one will be no different from the last three—citywide celebrations with no incidents of violence. More importantly in the long run, Beacon now possesses the means and community support necessary to address the root of community problems—long-term structural violence.

Entering a Dispute as Mediator

I. Building a Passport

Gaining access to a dispute is one of the most challenging tasks of peacemaking. To be a mediator requires a "passport" making you acceptable to both sides. Passports do not usually come free. Mostly mediators have to construct their own from one or all of the following four elements.

Reputations—personal or institutional. A reputation provides the easiest passport to a dispute. A reputation as a *mediator* is not essential. But if you intend to base your passport on your reputation, you do need a reputation for being fair, committed to meeting need, and impartial. This may be a personal reputation or the reputation of an institution with which you are associated.

If you are not already associated with an appropriate agency, perhaps you will need to link up with an existing institution which has the reputation you covet. What about asking the city Council of Churches to sponsor you? Or you may need to *create* an institutional base made up of reputable individuals or groups. What about organizing a "concerned citizens' group" including prominent community members or agencies?

Vouchers. Almost as good as a reputation are individuals or agencies who will vouch for your credibility. Who do you know who knows the disputing parties and can assure them that you are trustworthy? Can you find even one person well-based in the community who will listen to and understand your concerns? One sympathetic ear may open the way to more.

Forums. If you succeed in creating a forum for discussion or a joint task involving both sides, you will gain credibility. Will both sides send a representative to inform your church of the issues as they see them? Or will both send a member to a committee being formed to work on community problems? (See Chapter VIII.)

Resources. Provide resources parties see as serving their own interest and you may gain their confidence. For example, parties need to appear legitimate and fair-minded in the eyes of the community. Thus they may jump at a chance to "provide the facts of the matter" to anyone with channels to the community—reseacher, reporter, writer, representative of a concerned community group, etc. Or they may welcome the opportunity to demonstrate their fair-mindedness by presenting their views to a church or community group or by participating in a task force established by others.

Parties also need access to influential people. Are you in a position to provide it? Parties need expertise. Can you offer information they have overlooked or are too busy to locate? Can you help train them in negotiation or organizing? Parties need money or material aid. Can you locate any?

Naturally some of these needs raise questions of neutrality and intervenors need to consider carefully whether or not they intend to be entirely neutral and how locating resources will affect neutrality.

II. First Contacts

Regardless how you have built your passport, in your first contacts with parties as potential mediator there are several things **you are not trying to do.** You are not aiming to extract promises to cooperate, nor expecting an enthusiastic reception, nor seeking for intimate and confidential discussion on substantive issues. If these are offered or occur naturally, excellent. Receive the gift gratefully. But expect them and you will probably become disheartened. Push for them and you may be cold-shouldered.

You are looking for: 1) A chance to get acquainted; 2) opportunity to indicate you are talking with all sides and may be in a position to pass on ideas not currently being discussed; and 3) some indication of willingness to meet with you again. When these things have occurred, you are probably in a position to attempt a conscious role as a mediator. This does not mean that the parties trust you yet or view you as a mediator. It *does* mean that you have gotten over the initial hurdle of gaining access to the dispute.

What if a party refuses? Frequently one party will be so indignant and self-righteous at the behavior of the other they will refuse to even meet with them. "It won't do any good.... You just don't understand how perverse these folks are.... She's simply trying to harass me..., etc." Don't argue—you'll only increase the resistance. The goal is not to hard-sell mediation, but to get a foot in the door. Aim to propose something the party in question can agree to that will give you opportunity to meet with them again.

> I was once asked by the mayor of my home town to mediate an inter-personal dispute between two neighbors that had tied several municipal offices in knots for weeks. The one party agree to try mediation. But when I phoned the second, he immediately announced he had just sent a letter to the mayor, informing him that he was **not** interested in mediation. He had done nothing wrong, he said, and he refused to submit to further harassment by his neighbors.
>
> My heart sank—we were in the process of establishing a local mediation center and we needed the credibility that success in a case like this could help to build. Trying to avoid contradicting what he just said, I explained what happens in mediation. And I reminded that even if he had done no wrong, the harassment would probably continue if his neighbors remained angry with him. He was listening but was not convinced.
>
> Casting about for some way to end our conversation that

would leave open the possibility of further discussion, I finally said, "If I could get your neighbors to agree to stop harassing you, would you be willing to meet with them?" Without hesitating "Of course!" We discussed what it might take to convince the neighbors to make such a promise and then concluded with him urging me to contact him if I had any luck with the neighbors. I had my foot in the door!

Look for a legitimate goal that the resisting party seeks and connect that goal to mediation: "If I could..., would you be interested in discussing this further with me?" Obviously there are limits to this—mediation is more than manipulation! Obviously, too, you cannot guarantee success, but promise to give it a try. Whether you succeed or not, do report back to the individual or group. You may find that by the time you return, you will have earned some acceptance as a mediator.

III. Earning Trust: The Task That Never Ends

Trust is crucial to effectiveness as a mediator. Earning trust is most important at the entry stage, but maintaining it will preoccupy the mediator throughout. Rarely does he or she enjoy as much as might be desired. Security is not a part of the mediator's job description! Remember the following in earning trust:

1. **Accept vulnerability cheerfully and matter-of-factly as inherent to your task.** You will be more self-confident as a result and thus more able to inspire confidence. Besides, you'll live longer!

2. Parties will watch what you do with the information they give you. **Guard your knowledge carefully and use it with discretion.** (See Chapter X on mediating inter-personal disputes, noting particularly the "if-then" technique.)

3. Parties will be sensitive, especially in early contacts, to your response to their views. **Describe, don't evaluate.** Probably you will not agree with everything said, but you can still make it clear that you empathize with their problems and feelings.

4. Parties will test you with little tasks to see if you really can serve their own interests. **Be on the look-out for small tasks that need to be done and perform them well,** if you can do so without appearing partial.

5. When parties attack the unreasonableness of the demands of the other side (a theme which usually predominates in early discussion), **don't try to change opinions now.** Sometimes it is helpful to respond that a demand is simply one side's solution to a problem. Thus the challenge is to go beyond the demands to the underlying problem. How can the problem be resolved so that the unreasonable demands end? (See Chapter XII, p.86 for more on "Problem-Centeredness".) Later you may need to help each party see that the other is not so unreasonable as they appear. But it is more important to work at building trust between the mediator and the parties in early contacts than it is to change attitudes.

VIII / The Joint Task and the Discussion Forum

Often antagonism is so high that disputing parties are unwilling to hear of cooperation towards settlement. By creating a "Joint Task" or a "Discussion Forum," peacemakers can sometimes nevertheless contribute towards communication, even if parties are unwilling to consider direct negotiation.

Discussion Forum in a Housing Dispute

When a housing dispute developed in my home town, I was part of a group of people who gathered once a month to discuss issues relevant to Christian faith. The dispute had been simmering for several months—over whether or not to convert an abandoned warehouse into housing for low and middle income families.

There were three visible parties in the dispute. Residents of the neighborhood were strongly opposed to the project because, they said, it would make the neighborhood congested. The organization proposing to do the renovation insisted their proposal would give excellent use to the building and up-grade the neighborhood. The city Bureau of Housing was not taking a position either way, but had previously stated concern about a shortage of housing in the area.

Our discussion group was primarily interested in an education about the issues related to housing in the city, since we are urban Christians. We decided to invite a representative from each of the three parties involved—the neighborhood, the non-profit housing corporation, and the city—to present their views to us on this particular conflict. We phoned each of the parties and found all three of them most eager to present their case. It didn't seem to matter very much to any of them that they did not know of our existence before or that we were small. We stressed that they would need to keep their presentations short (five to ten minutes) so that we would have time for questions and discussion.

The meeting was a surprising experience, for us and for them. There had been some quite heated exchanges among the parties in previous meetings. Thus we were not sure what would happen in this session. However, the presence of 30 concerned but impartial individuals in the room, there simply out of personal and moral interest in the community, seemed to provide a reservoir of good will. This set an atmosphere for open and reasonable discussion. The parties were all good-natured and matter-of-fact in their presentations. There was even an occasional laughing jibe.

To the surprise of everyone, there were numerous times when one party or the other said, "We didn't realize that's what you were saying. We thought you were planning to..." There was also an exchange of information that opened some chances for cooperation.

For example, one of the reasons the neighbors cited for opposing the housing was lack of adequate street parking space. The area is already over-parked, they asserted. However, someone in our group pointed out that one of the main reasons for over-parking was the presence of a local industry. Although workers at the plant had access to a company parking lot, many of them chose to park on the street in the neighborhood, to avoid lines at the parking lot. This provided the housing corporation opportunity to pledge that they would make every possible effort to see that only neighborhood residents be allowed to park on the streets. The city had a program for issuing residential permits only to neighbors in such situations.

The dispute has gone before the zoning board and the outcome remains unclear. I have stayed in touch with the parties since in exchanging some ideas. What impressed me about the discussion was the rapid credibility which that meeting provided our group with the three parties. We gave each equal air time and they appreciated the chance to express their views. It was clear to them that we were relatively impartial and genuinely committed to the needs of the community. Effort on our part was minimal, yet that one hour forum provided us with good access to the dispute, and enough credibility to pursue on-going relationships as a potential mediator.

Joint Task in a Racial Conflict

In his book *American Dreams: Lost and Found,* author Studs Terkel (Pantheon Books, 1980) presents an inspiring example of a joint task bringing antagonists together. Terkel interviewed C.P. Ellis, a former Klansman and once president of the local chapter of the Ku Klux Klan in Durham, North Carolina. Ellis describes in humorous detail his involve-ment in the KKK, beginning with his initiation when he promised to "uphold the purity of the white race, fight communism, and protect white womanhood." Before long Ellis had risen to the office of President or "Exalted Cyclops."

As head of the Durham Klan, Ellis was an aggressive leader. The Civil Rights Movement was reaching the peak of its activities and Ellis and his Klansmen reacted zealously. They began staging open confrontations with blacks in community meetings. They began courting the friendship of City Councilmen and county commissioners, visiting some city leaders in their homes. "It wasn't long," Ellis recalls, "before councilmen would call me up: 'The blacks are comin' up tonight and makin' outrageous demands. How about some of you people showin' up and have a little balance?' "

Ellis and his supporters would gather and fill up half the council chambers. Blacks filled the other half and invariably the two groups ended up quarreling.

With a laugh, Ellis recalls the person he despised most at the time. "I never will forget some black lady I hated with purple passion. Ann Atwater. Everytime I'd go downtown, she'd be leadin' a boycott. How I hated her!"

Then an amazing thing happened. The State AFL-CIO received a grant from the Federal Government to tackle racial problems in the school system. Ellis received a phone call from the President of the AFL-CIO. "We'd like to get some people together from all walks of life," he said. Would Ellis care to join them? Ellis was hostile: "Who you talkin' about?" "Blacks, whites, liberals, conservatives, Klansmen, NAACP people," came the response. Ellis refused.

But then a White Citizens' Council Member dropped by and said, "Let's go up there and see what's goin' on. It's tax money bein' spent." They went. Ellis laughs at the memory of the scene that met his skeptical eyes. Blacks, white liberals, and—who else—Ann Atwater. "I just forced myself to go in and sit down," Ellis recollects.

Ellis sat and listened to charges of white racism until he could take no more. Then he asked for the floor and cut loose. The problem, he remembers asserting, was black racism. If there weren't blacks in the schools, the schools wouldn't have the problems they had.

Then Howard Clements, a black man, stood up. "I will never forget," says Ellis. "I'm certainly glad C.P. Ellis come," Clements began, "because he's the most honest man here tonight." Ellis chuckles as he remembers his reaction at the time: "What's that nigger tryin' to do?"

But the meeting had an impact on Ellis. "I got some things off my chest," he recalls. The group continued meeting. At the third meeting, the group elected committees and then agreed to elect two chairpersons. Then came yet another shock. Joe Beckton, director of the Human Relations Commission and "just as black as he can be" nominated Ellis. Other blacks objected. Then someone nominated Ann Atwater as co-chairperson. "Ain't no way I can work with that gal," Ellis remembers thinking. But finally he agreed to accept, weary of fighting.

There they were, a Klansman and a militant black woman, co-chairmen of the school committee. "It was impossible. How could I work with her?" Ellis remembers thinking. Ann Atwater felt the same way, he recalls. But something about the challenge appealed to Ellis. It gave him a sense of belonging, a feeling of pride. "This helped this inferiority feeling I had." Reluctantly they began working together.

48

A turning point came one night when Ellis called Atwater on the phone. "Ann," he said, "you and I should have a lot of differences and we got 'em now. But there's somethin' laid out here before us, and if it's gonna be a success, you and I are gonna have to make it one. Can we lay aside some of these feelins?" Atwater's response was firm. "I'm willing if you are." They agreed to try.

The change in Ellis' heart did not occur overnight. His friends resisted these new activities. He changed jobs. He and Ann began knocking on doors in their respective communities, talking with people. Both received hostile responses at times. To Ellis came the charge, "You're sellin' us out, Ellis, get out of my door. I don't want to talk to you." Ann got the angry accusation, "What are you doin' messin' with that Klansman?"

One day Ellis and Atwater went back to school and sat down to talk. Ann said, "My daughter came home cryin' everyday. She said her teacher was makin' fun of me in front of the other kids." "The same thing happened to my kid," said Ellis. "White liberal teacher was makin' fun of Tim Ellis' father, the Klansman. In front of other peoples. He came home cryin'." In that moment, Ellis recalls, he began to see that although he and Ann were of very different backgrounds, their problems were identical, "except hers bein' black and me bein' white." The revelation was startling. "From that moment on, I tell ya', that gal and I worked together good."

Their efforts continued. Ellis and Atwater came up with resolutions, formed with the help of many community people, which the school system rejected. Ellis then decided to run for school board membership. He lost, but the experience carried him further in the direction he was moving.

He returned to school and got his high school diploma. Then he became active in union organizations. Today he is the regional business manager of the International Union of Operating Engineers. With pride in his voice he recalls his bid for the position of Business Manager of the union. He invited some of his old black friends to speak on his behalf. Howard Clements teased a bit: "I don't know what I'm doin' here, supporting an ex-Klansman," but then he said, "I know what C.P. Ellis come from. I knew him when he was. I knew him as he grew, and growed with him. I'm tellin' you now: follow, follow this Klansman." In a union whose membership is 75% black, Ellis won his office, four votes to every one.

Conflict
Between
Individuals

A moderate level of conflict is not only inevitable in interpersonal encounters, but it can actually enhance a relationship. "First, it may allow new motivation and energy to be discovered by the conflicting parties. Second, the innovation of individuals may be heightened due to a perceived necessity to deal with the conflict. Third, each individual in the conflict situation can develop an increased understanding of his own perceptions by having to articulate his views in a conflicting and argumentative situation. Fourth, each person often develops a firmer sense of identity; conflict allows values and belief systems to emerge into fuller view."

> —Richard Walton as summarized in Ronald C. Arnett,
> **Dwell in Peace** (The Brethren Press), p. 70

IX / Personal Skills

Peacemaking is in the end a very personal task. The ability to enjoy oneself among others, to welcome the challenge of differences, and to communicate in spite of them is crucial to the peacemaker. Good mediators are usually also good friends, spouses, and colleagues.

The first section describes obstacles to peace which I have learned first-hand from my own teachers—individuals who created and are in some cases still maintaining those obstacles. (Yes, myself included!) The second and third sections examine attitudes and skills that support resolution of disputes at the personal level.

Eight Ways to Turn Disagreements Into Feuds

Disputes are a cinch to create and maintain. Not that all disagreements inevitably become nasty conflicts. On the contrary, disagreements often lead to greater harmony and communication. But having spent many hours working with people who are at odds, it has become clear to me that the tactics that keep disputes alive and festering are really quite simple. Simple, that is, if you follow a few simple principles.

For the benefit of others, I have set down these principles on paper. Anyone can add a bit of color to an unfulfilled life by mastering the following suggestions for turning disagreements into bitter feuds.

1. Easily the most potent tool for ensuring a life well-scarred by disputes is to develop and maintain a healthy fear of conflict. This will do several things.

For one, it will prevent others from knowing that concerns exist on your part until long after they originate. It will keep you from developing a direct and healthy relationship with your friends. It will guarantee that if and when you do discuss problems with them, you will be upset and in an explosive frame of mind. Consequently, your friends will inevitably be baffled, defensive, and indignant at your out-of-proportion emotions. They will quickly conclude that you are "out to get them" and will soon find additional evidence from current incidents and memories of previous encounters to bolster their conclusion. You will be well on your way to making your friends opponents.

Better yet, assume that those individuals about whom you are disturbed do not wish to discuss things face-to-face, that they probably intend to do you harm or take as much as they can get at your expense. It is clear that trying to talk with them about things will do no good! Remember too, that if perchance they do intend no harm, they will be absolutely crushed, their world thrown into total chaos, if you share honestly with them that you need to talk with them about some things that disturb you.

Best of all—and I have yet to see this variation on fear of conflict fail—tell everyone except the offending party about your concerns. You know that it would do no good anyway to discuss the situation directly with the individual involved, so rally others to your side while you can.

This is the first and greatest commandment of conflict maintenance.

2. If perchance you do get in a situation where you are discussing a conflict with the other party involved, be as vague as possible about the issues. That is, avoid stating your concerns in such a way that the other party can do anything practical to change the situation. Use generalities like, "you are arrogant," "you're self-seeking and materialistic," "you're just jealous," "you're insensitive to others," "you're the most unChristian person I know," etc. To keep the dispute festering you must *not* speak in specifics like this: "It made me feel ignored and angry when you cut down all the trees on our common boundary without approaching me first," or "I felt like you completely misundestood me when you slammed the door in my face and then hung up the phone."

3. The third commandment of conflict maintenance is to assume that you know all the facts of the matter and that they clearly indicate that you are right. After all, there is only one sensible way to interpret a situation. You know that you are honest, intelligent, and successful in other matters. You also know that you are not malicious. Obviously then, you are right and the other side is wrong. Clinch your position if possible by finding a Bible verse to *prove* you are right!

One good way of learning how to effectively use self-righteousness to prevent resolution of disputes is to watch your children. Note how readily they lay all blame on others when they disagree. They see what they wish to see and really *do* believe it was the other's fault! You can easily do the same, and achieve the same results.

Remember, too, that if and when discussion occurs you must speak prophetically for truth. There is no room for "prophetic listening"—that would only allow the other side to strengthen their distorted notions and cast doubt upon what you know to be true. Insist on doing most of the talking and none of the listening and you will quite handily stifle any possibility of dialogue. Your opponent will depart thinking you are a scoundrel and feeling like a wretch (of course you knew him as that from the very start).

4. An effective variation, particularly useful in those situations where a rather unassertive person is upset with you, is to announce that you will talk with anyone who wishes to discuss problems with you—then let it be known that your responsibility ends there. Do this with just a touch of defiance and you can rest assured that the other party will conclude that it is useless to talk with you anyway.

Recall here a peacemaker famed, among other things, for initiating reconciliation of his own people with other races. Jesus of Nazareth once remarked that those who know others are upset with them should initiate dialogue with the aggrieved (Matthew 5:23-26). Clearly then, you should do exactly the opposite and leave the entire burden of reconciliation upon the offended party.

5. Latch onto whatever evidence you can find—count on it, you'll always be able to find some—showing that the main problem is the other party is jealous of you. Thus, you can rest assured that your opponent is merely trying to harass you. You need not take him or her seriously, nor heed the concerns of others who may approach you. Probably you are the only one in a position to understand the jealous and vengeful aspects of his nature. You are above engaging in discussion about petty games.

6. Judge the motivation of the other party on the basis of one or two mistakes on their part. Forget that everyone makes mistakes. Forget that even the best-intentioned person may demonstrate unkindness in a conflict. Instead, find one or two incidents which your opponent handled wrongly and use that as proof that he or she is malicious.

Perhaps the best time to apply this principle is just after initial discussion about the disagreement has gotten underway. Both of you will be grasping for some explanation for this troublesome dispute. At this stage, you will find it particularly easy to latch onto a failure, an angry word, a broken promise from the other party as proof for what you suspected all along—the guy really *is* a scoundrel.

7. If all these conflict maintaining mechanisms fail and, despite your best efforts, you find yourself engaging in discussion with your opponent, approach resolution as a strictly win/lose situation. That is, view this as a situation where one person must win and the other person must lose.

It's either him or you! Keep your options for settlement as few as possible. In this manner, both of you will be in a proper frame of mind to reject out-of-hand everything the other proposes.

What you don't want is a situation where both of you are committed to a win for everyone and dignity on all sides. Avoid brainstorming about various alternatives. Avoid uncritical listing of possible solutions. Get too many options lying on the table, and you might find yourselves bargaining towards an agreement which leaves everyone satisfied!

8. Your last line of recourse, if somehow a proposal is brought to you that might resolve the dispute, is to respond that you are not in a

position to negotiate. Your spouse, your business partner, or maybe your bank has to be in on the discussion. Don't get weaseled into promising to advocate a given solution. Simply pass the buck by saying you are not in a position to commit yourself to anything. Even if you can't avoid discussion, it's a cinch to avoid negotiating in good faith!

*   *   *   *   *   *   *

There you have it folks. Master these principles in one dispute, and you will find it easier to get involved in others as well. Those interested in avoiding change and growth in personal relationships should find these principles particularly helpful. A few simmering disputes will in time differentiate bland souls with obvious scars. It'll make them real characters!

One last tip—avoid mediators, particularly the Christian peacemakers—they have a way of bringing healing in even the nastiest of disputes!

Attitudes Are Crucial

Two neighbors had problems with a common driveway. Rather than discuss problems openly as they arose, both shied from confrontation, avoiding each other as much as possible. With resentment and frustration bottled up on both sides, in time the entire relationship became polarized over the driveway. Things at last became intolerable and one neighbor finally approached the other. Just as he had expected, he was met with a barrage of hostile words. Convinced now his neighbor was irresponsible and unreasonable, the man returned home and ordered a fence built splitting the driveway.

Conflict *avoidance* is probably the greatest threat to harmonious relationships. Conflict *prevention*, a positive effort to foresee conflict and resolve it with clear communication and planning, is a worthy goal. But *avoidance* is different. Avoidance is passive and negative, reducing communication to escape the symptoms of conflict without addressing the causes. Avoidance almost always increases the long-term pain and disruption of conflict.

There is a reason for this. Where resentment is bottled up, deep-seated personal hostility usually develops and parties come to view each other as irresponsible, uncaring, dishonest, or worse. Issues and problems, such as who parks where, are resolvable. But personal antagonisms are hard to change.

To summarize in a rule with few exceptions: **Conflict avoidance makes resolution much harder by shifting the focus of attention from issues, which are manageable, to personal antagonisms, which are explosive.**

Conflict becomes less threatening when individuals develop proper attitudes toward conflict. The neighbors above probably would have gotten together much earlier and resolved their difficulties quickly if they had taken the following attitudes towards conflict.

1. Conflict is neither good nor bad. Rather it is a tool whose outcome depends on how it is used.

2. Conflict is constructive when it leads toward needed change (justice), and recognizes and enhances the dignity of all involved.

3. The goal of conflict resolution is not to avoid or necessarily to reduce conflict, but to channel it constructively.

Since conflict is a tool that can lead to good or bad, it is essential to develop skill in using conflict to bring good. One reason people become fearful of conflict and fall into a pattern of avoidance is they do not know *how* to handle conflict constructively. There *are* skills and strategies that can be taught and learned that help make conflict a constructive experience.

Towards Disagreeing Constructively

I. Skills: Develop *communication skills* that bring genuine exchange with others in disagreement.

A. **Recognize your anger and express it appropriately**—i.e.: at the time and place of provocation if possible; *not* days or weeks later, *not* displaced onto another person.

B. **Communicate with "I-messages."** Reduce defensiveness in others by speaking in terms of your own feelings and needs.

> Examples: I felt as though you didn't respect my intelligence when....
> It would make things so much easier for me if you would....
> I don't understand fully what's happening between us, but I've been deeply hurt by some things you've done recently....
> NOT: You totally disregard my feelings and act like you think I'm a fool....
> You have got to stop....
> You're obnoxious and unkind....

The most effective "I-Messages" state: 1) the feelings of the speaker, 2) the objectionable behavior, and 3) the consequences of the objectionable behavior on the speaker. Example: "I get irritated when you arrive late day after day because it upsets my schedule for the rest of the morning"

C. **Use questions honestly**, to understand and learn, not to manipulate. "The most frequently misused communication pattern is the question. In fact, most questions are pseudo-questions—coercive opinions, statements or views offered in concealed ways." (Dave Augsburger)
AVOID: *The Cooptive Question*—Limits or restricts the possible

response of the other. "Don't you think that...?" "Isn't it true that...?"

The Punitive Question—"Why did you do, say, try that?"

The Command Question—When are you going to do something about...?

The Set-Up Question—Maneuvers the other into a vulnerable position, ready for the axe. "Is it true that you...?" "Didn't you say that...?"

D. **State concerns in "Workable Problem Statements."** I.e.: Speak in a way that the other person can *do* something about what you're saying. Refer to specific actions or incidents: who, what, to whom, when, where?

> Example: I feel hurt when you suggest to your friends that as a woman, I'm not as smart as you.
> NOT: You're a chauvinist.

> Example: It made me very resentful of you when you criticized me with six other people nearby.
> NOT: You don't care how I feel, do you?

> Example: You are not providing equal employment opportunity. We would like to see you hire 3 black employees within the next 12 months.
> NOT: You're a bunch of racists.

E. **Use "reflective listening."** Listen for what the person speaking is *feeling* and play back those feelings. When someone attacks you verbally, instead of responding defensively, try: "You're feeling really upset with me, because..." The aim is to let the other person know that you recognize what they are feeling, rather than to put up barriers against their feelings. "It's clear I made you feel badly when I..."

II. Tactics: Structure your discussion in such a way that you can discuss conflicts as a joint problem. Try the following sequence:

A. **Define the problems.** Each party states the problem in terms of their own need in "I-Messages" form (see I-B above).

B. **List the criteria for a solution.** What conditions must a solution meet to satisfy both parties? Example: "Our solution should keep our joint driveway open so A can get to his house unobstructed; allow B to use the drive occasionally for guest parking; enable us to discuss future problems as they occur." Prioritize the criteria. (Alternative: Re-state problem so as to include the needs of both parties. For example: "The problem is that A needs to have free access to his house and B needs to have parking space for visitors."

C. **List several solutions.** Brainstorm and list as many as possible, from the practical to the absurd, before evaluating.

D. **Evaluate solutions against criteria.** Discard the most unacceptable.

E. **Develop the best solution** combining the features of several alternatives.

III. Tips: Remember the following as you work towards resolution.

A. The key to successful resolution is **satisfying the perceived needs** of all parties.

B. **Saving face and self-respect are crucial.** Find ways for the other party to save face and they will take your needs seriously. Support their self-respect and the agreement will be a lasting one. When you win a point, credit the other party for their sincerity and fair-mindedness.

C. **Deal with issues sequentially.** Avoid drifting from one point of contention to another without really resolving any. If possible, discuss each issue until everyone is satisfied, and *then* move on to other problems. This keeps discussion manageable.

D. **Start with the easiest issues.** Success in small items will give you momentum in tackling larger ones.

E. The more frequently **yes, no, and why (why not)** appear in your discussion, the better, for they are the marks of direct, problem-focused discussion.

F. If you cannot agree on anything else, at least **agree to meet again.** Commitment to continue working at problems is genuine progress. Besides, time brings amazing changes.

Additional Reading: For more information on "Active Listening" and "I-Messages," see Gordon Thompson's **Parent Effectiveness Training** *(Wyden, 1970). Dave Augsburger's* **The Love Fight: Caring Enough to Confront** *(Herald Press, 1973) is helpful and concise.* **Looking Out/Looking In** *by Adler and Town. (Holt, Rinehart and Winston, 1978) is an excellent college text on interpersonal skills.*

X / A Procedure for Mediating Inter-Personal Disputes

John Miller was disturbed and anxious. As deacon of his church, he had been bothered for several years by a series of incidents involving David Horst, a farmer in his congregation. The lane to Horst's farm extended half a mile beyond his buildings to two other farms, and the owners of those farms used the lane several times daily. No problem there—everyone knew that an easement was written into the deed of David's farm when he bought the land, a clause giving the other farmers legal right to use David's lane. The problem was that no one had ever stated who should pay up-keep on the lane. Misunderstandings had been present from the very beginning and had grown with the years. Whatever willingness may have once existed to discuss things cooperatively had now disappeared in the heat of numerous nasty confrontations. The most recent incident was an attempt by David a month ago to block the lane, followed promptly a few days later by a skunk in his mailbox. Tempers were high and both sides were consulting lawyers.

*Miller felt keenly a responsibility to help resolve the dispute, but he felt almost paralyzed to begin. Horst had been avoiding him at church lately and would be skeptical of any peacemaking efforts. "They're just a bunch of liars!" he had once commented about the other farmers. Nor did Miller know how he would proceed even if Horst agreed to cooperate. He was not at all sure he could keep face-to-face discussion within reason. He had to do **something** sooner or later, but **what** he did not know.*

One of the toughest problems for peacemakers is bringing disputing parties into a conflict resolution process. Often the same factors which create a dispute cause the disputing parties to resist mediation attempts—fear of conflict, suspicion of motivations, or a genuine belief that discussion will do no good.

Trust in the third-party peacemaker is the most effective tool in overcoming resistance among the disputing parties. A reputation is invaluable, but not everyone interested in peacemaking possesses one. Connections with a church, or links with a network of individuals interested and skilled in conflict resolution can provide credibility. Small, informal "mediation centers," provide an established base for mediation in some communities. (See also Chapter VII on "Entering Disputes".)

Nevertheless, most individuals committed to conflict resolution will find themselves in a position where they will have to either *create* a base for their efforts or else approach conflicts simply as concerned individuals. Patience and common sense are the best resources in this situation. Still, there is a force active in most conflicts which can add to whatever other forces of good will the peacemaker can rally to the cause.

Use Self-Righteousness to the Advantage of Peace

Unless genuinely skeptical of the mediator's motivations, which may well be the case initially, most individuals in a dispute are eager to talk. Even the best of humans are somewhat self-righteous in disputes. This fact stands the peacemaker in good stead in gaining entry, since self-righteous people are usually eager to convince others of the "facts" of the matter. Thus often merely stating a concern, displaying a genuine willingness to listen and be educated about the dispute is all that it takes for a mediator to elicit lengthy rumination from one or both parties in a dispute. The question, "Can you help me understand what's happening here?" can open many doors if sincerely asked.

Self-righteousness will later become an obstacle to be contended with. I have worked with Christians on opposite sides of a dispute, both of whom had received a "special word from the Lord" justifying their position—that "word" happened to be two directly contradictory words!

But in the beginning, use self-righteousness in the interests of the peacemaking process by accepting it unchallenged. You will earn an education about the issues in dispute. You may also win trust on both sides. Later, when mediation is actually under way, you may need to undermine self-righteousness in private caucus—and probably by then will have the credibility to do so.

Who Should Be There?

Save time and frustration by making sure that everyone crucial to resolution is present. Try to gain a sense for who has been genuinely antagonized or antagonistic. Often this involves more than one person on each side of the dispute. For example, if two couples are at odds, the husbands may feel things will be more readily resolved if just the two of them work things out, without their wives to complicate matters. But if the wives have shared deeply in the antagonism, and have strong personal opinions about the dispute, they need to be present for reconciliation as well, even if it means the process is more complicated and difficult.

As a rule, the fewer the number of people involved in a mediation session, the more manageable the process and the more likely a solution. But someone who has had personal stakes in the dispute, and is likely to veto a resolution in which they have not had a hand, should be included in the process.

* * * * * * *

Once disputing parties are brought to the mediation, there are four stages through which most successful mediation sessions must run. These are: I. Introduction; II. Story-telling; III. Problem-solving; IV. Agreement.

Beginning with the Introduction, let us examine these stages in detail.

I. Introduction

The opening minutes are crucial. The disputing parties come with a history of poor communication; they are distrustful both of each other and of what may happen here. The only thing making this meeting different from previous unsuccessful communication attempts is the presence of a mediator. Thus the parties will look, and rightly so, to the mediator to provide a sense of reason, fairness, and control. The mediator must begin things with a sense of purpose and order, without being pompous or officious.

In addition to setting a problem-solving mood, the mediator does several things in the introduction. He or she indicates how the session will run so there will be no surprises. He or she sets ground rules for the discussion so the parties need not fear that communication will get out of hand. And lastly, the mediator clarifies his or her own role in the process.

What To Include

Here is a checklist of things that should be covered in the introductory statement by the mediator.

1. Personal introductions as necessary.

2. Indicate what will happen in the session. Explain that you will ask each party to present their story from their own perspective and then state what they wish to happen in this session. After that you will be trying to find areas of agreement. Explain that you may be caucusing with one or both parties from time to time; that is, you will be meeting privately with each party occasionally. What is said in caucus is confidential unless agreed otherwise.

3. Establish the basic ground rule. Each party will be given opportunity to tell their story *uninterrupted*. You may wish to add other ground rules depending on the situation. If you fear anger will get out of hand, you may ask the parties to agree to set anger aside and deal fairly with the issues.

4. Clarify your own role as mediator. You are not a judge, you cannot make decisions for the parties. They themselves must work out the agreement. You are simply here to facilitate *their* agreement. You are not interested in declaring guilt or innocence—you are only interested in helping the parties find a solution that both can live with. The mediation process is a process of "exchanging promises about the future in order to resolve a dispute now." Your task is simply to help exchange those promises.

II. Story-telling: Presentations of Stories and Expectations

Turn now to one of the parties—normally the one that has initiated the complaint—and ask them to tell the story of the dispute as they experienced it. They should assume that you, the mediator, know nothing and aim to include the following:

1. Describe exactly how you are feeling,
2. When did this start?
3. Who or what caused this?
4. Why did he, she or it do this? By accident? On purpose?

Half of the value of this "story-telling" is the opportunity for each side to hear the whole situation presented uninterrupted from another viewpoint. Usually that is a new experience for everyone!

Ventilation

Be prepared for some anger to emerge as the parties relive experiences from the past. Strong emotion is fine, as long as it is not expressed in insulting ways, and as long as it does not provoke an escalating exchange of hostility between the two parties. Some "ventilation" now may help the parties to get hostility out of their system, and move on towards resolution in later stages. In fact, you may at times wish to encourage ventilation by asking parties to describe their feelings during an incident they are relating.

Keeping It Manageable

Probably you will need to remind both parties more than once that everyone will get a chance to state their views and that each person will be allowed to speak uninterrupted. No need to be legalistic about enforcing the rule—a spontaneous exchange here and there may speed the process of getting down to real issues. But see to it that in general the rule prevails.

Note reactions by parties not speaking. If it's clear that listeners are having a very difficult time keeping silent, perhaps you can prevent an angry walk-out by interrupting the speaker with: "It's clear not everyone agrees with you and we'll try to hear how the others feel about this after you're finished."

Listening

If it was important for the mediator to be a model of candor, reason, and fairness during the introduction, it is doubly important that the mediator now become a model listener. The importance of careful and sympathetic listening cannot be stressed enough. From now until the time that final agreement is reached, the primary role for the mediator to fill is that of a good listener. Naturally the mediator must speak periodically. But when the mediator speaks, it is mainly as a listener, as someone who is trying to gain more information or better understanding.

Listen for facts. Listen for feelings, both expressed and unexpressed. Listen for specific demands. Listen for offers of "deals" which may slip out without fanfare ("Maybe I'd pay back his loan if he would stop talking about it behind my back"). Make notes as you listen so you don't lose the things you're hearing.

Make it *clear* you are listening. Use eye contact. a nod of the head. an occasional "mm-hmm" to indicate sympathy and close attention. "Active" or "reflective" listening skills are especially useful here. (See p. 58. See also Thomas Gordon's book, *Leadership Effectiveness Training* (Wyden Books, 1977), pp. 54-70).

Getting All the Issues Out Onto the Table

Not infrequently. if you have spoken with both sides privately at some length about the situation before the mediation session. the parties will only mention briefly or totally ignore those one or two events or feelings which anger them the most. These are incidents which probably are threatening to both parties to discuss and if you know something about them already. the parties may take the easy way out and avoid discussing them. Of course, it is precisely these incidents or feelings which are most crucial to the discussion. Note the omission of any crucial events or perceptions and help the parties get everything out on the table by asking to be filled in on these matters.

Digging to the Root of Conflict

Probably the most important thing to listen for at this story-telling stage is *why*. Successful resolution will have to get to the root of problems and deal with underlying causes. You will likely need to dig for these causes and bring them out into the open. without seeming to interrogate either party. Ask your questions sympathetically. Be careful about asking direct "why?" questions. Instead, use broader responses that will elicit further reflection in areas that you feel are critical—"Tell me more about that" or "Say more about what was behind that" or "So you felt that was really unfair."

Turning Toward Solutions

After the first party has told their story. ask them to say what they want to happen in this session. This statement may bring out additional issues that did not come through in the story and it will give you a place from which to begin in finding agreement.

Repeat the process with the second party. After both sides have presented their story ask if either party has clarifying questions to ask. It may be necessary to remind the parties that they have already had opportunity to present their own viewpoint. Thus you are interested. not in a re-statement of things already said. but in questions clarifying facts about each side's viewpoint.

Sometimes disputes are resolved at this point. It's amazing how many disputes are based on simple ignorance of what the other side wants. Getting things out in the open may "clear the air" and put everyone in a mood for resolving things quickly. If this has happened. agreement will not be difficult to reach. But more likely, you will find that although tension is somewhat reduced, the real challenge of mediation is just now beginning.

II. Problem-Solving: Working Towards Resolution

The "story-telling" stage is often characterized by hostility, competitiveness, and self-righteousness. For resolution to occur, parties must move beyond this stage. Rarely will disputants make this transition easily or completely. Frequently the mediator must struggle throughout to move conflicting parties towards the "Problem-solving" stage.

Shifting Towards Problem-solving

Once story-telling and statements of expectations are completed, you can help turn the mood towards "adult" problem-solving by doing the following.

1. Summarize the "story" of each disputant. "Mr. Jones, if I'm understanding you rightly.. you're upset because.... Is that a fair summary of your concerns?" "Mr. Smith, you're saying that.... Have I gotten it correctly?"

2. Inquire if the parties are ready now to concentrate on finding solutions to the disagreement. This may help the parties to make a conscious transition in their minds.

3. Focus the issues. Begin if you can by reminding the parties of areas where they *agree* or need each other. After all, they both agree they'd like to resolve the problem, they both agree past incidents would be upsetting to anyone, they do need to be able to cooperate as neighbors....

Then list the areas needing to be resolved. "Let's list the areas in which we need to work out an understanding, 1) The incident that took place a year ago; 2) How to divide up expenses incurred in repairing the damaged property; 3) Who is responsible for over-all up-keep?; 4) What to do when concerns arise in the future?" *Have the parties list these areas themselves if you sense cooperation.*

From this point, attention focuses on dialogue between the two parties. The less intervention on your part, the better. If cooperation is good, all that may be required is a question to one or both parties—"What will it take to resolve these issues?— to initiate discussion that will eventually lead to an agreement.

But more likely you will need to provide additional help along the way. Matters may begin bogging down into much heated talk and no listening. Discussion will flit from one issue to another, with no progress on any item. Individuals will begin circling back to things already said earlier, repeating them again.

Deal With One Issue at a Time

When you are discussing one issue or incident and another is brought up, note the issue raised and assure the individual raising it that you will discuss that problem. But unless that issue demands priority over the issue currently in question, set it aside for the moment.

Help the Parties to Hear Each Other

One way to increase communication if it seems that neither party is listening to the other is to frequently summarize and clarify what you think each party is saying. Each party will listen to your feed-back of his *own* position and thus likely extend the same attention to your description of the other party's position.

A more drastic technique is "Rogerian Repetition." Before speaking, each individual must repeat what the previous speaker said, until the previous speaker is satisfied that his or her point has been accurately stated. The effect can be almost startling!

Call A Caucus

The caucus is a powerful tool in the mediator's kit of techniques. Very simply, it is a time when the mediator works separately with each party in private discussion. Parties may be unwilling to demonstrate any flexibility in the presence of other parties, particularly if the conflict is an old or highly competitive one. Caucus enables each party to consider compromise and to reflect on ways to meet the needs of the other party, in a no-risk environment.

Limitations of the Caucus

The caucus is often indispensable, but use it with caution. Some mediators, indeed, feel that it should not be used at all, because it perpetuates indirect communication. The major cause of many disputes, these mediators argue, is lack of direct communication between the parties. A mediator who relies heavily on caucuses and shuttle diplomacy thus fails to lay the groundwork for improved direct communication in the future.

There is truth, undoubtedly, in this viewpoint. Long-term direct communication is always the goal of the peacemaker. However, often parties are so locked into the dynamics of a specific dispute that when it comes to discussion of the hard issues of resolution, the old irrationality and personal resentment set in, preventing effective communication. A mediator working privately in caucus can repeatedly remind each party of the viewpoint of the other side, without getting drawn into the dynamics that prevent resolution. Successful resolution of one dispute frequently clears the air and paves the way for direct communication in the future.

If the mediator is sensitive to these limitations, the caucus will stand him or her in good service as a peacemaker.

Procedure in Caucus

Begin caucus by asking for feed-back from the party you are meeting with. For example: "How do you feel about what has happened so far?" "Are there important things that aren't being said?"

Then focus on solutions. "What is it going to take to resolve this?" The challenge at hand is to find and build common ground.

Seeking Common Ground

The goal of mediation is to find common ground between two parties and on the common ground to build an agreement. Where possible, the mediator builds common ground in the presence of both parties. Where the going is tough, caucus nevertheless enables the mediator to work towards finding common ground. In caucus the mediator confirms those areas of common ground that seem to be emerging; probes for additional areas that may not yet have appeared; discusses solutions for those areas where there is little or no common ground.

As you move between the parties, ask yourself these three questions to help sort out the jumble of information and emotions into useful facts:

1. In what areas do the parties already have common ground—common needs and interests? Take pains to discuss this with both parties—it will help clarify what you already know and, more important, focus the attention of the disputing parties on commonalities. Frequently parties are in a rut where only differences appear; thus they need repeated reminders of areas where they do stand together.

2. Where do I need to find common ground in order to make agreement possible? Ask questions until you can define in your own mind in concrete terms what common ground is lacking, until you have some idea of what it will take to resolve things.

3. Where or from whom can I get that? Answering this question is the biggest challenge of mediation. Doing so demands give-and-take from the parties. Now is the time for patience and endurance from everyone. The mediator's job is to find out what is important to each party and what is not-so-important and thus pave the way for agreement. Very quickly, you will discover that you know more than either party about the whole situation. From this position of greater knowledge you will be able to assist in creating common ground.

Finding Offers

If the key issues are difficult and complex, create a cooperative mood by finding agreement on lesser issues. One way to do this is to listen carefully for those things that are not-so-important to each party. Then convert those items into offers! That is, help each party to convert the things they are willing to give up into an offer in exchange for something they want.

Prioritizing Offers

Remember that the exchange of offers involves a bargaining process. Thus allow leeway for bargaining on key issues. Labor mediators sometimes help each disputing side to work out "first", "fall-back", and "final" offers. A "first" offer involves minimal compromise from the party making the offer in exchange for something desired from the other party. If the other party rejects the "first offer", a "fall-back" or later a "final offer" is made, each involving greater compromise. The community dispute mediator normally is not so detailed, but the same principle applies.

Exchanging Offers—The "If...Then Proposal"

As you meet with parties, ideas and offers for resolution will be offered. How will you introduce these to the other side? Use the "if... then" proposal.

Suppose that in caucus with one of the parties, it becomes clear that they are prepared to make major concessions in one of the areas being discussed. The mediator cannot simply go to the other party and say, "Mr. Jones has decided to reduce his request for damage repairs from $100 to $50." Mr. Jones needs to gain something in exchange for his offer.

Rather, the mediator looks for something desirable to Mr. Jones and then puts the two together in "if... then" form. "Mr. Smith, if Mr. Jones would reduce his request from $100 to $50, then would you consider...?" The proposal may be attractive to Mr. Smith. It may also be unacceptable. Probably he will want to modify it. In any case, the mediator will have been able to test out common ground without revealing the bottom line of either side or committing anyone to a particular position without them gaining anything in return.

When You Reach An Impasse—The "Reality-Tester"

As you are working to uncover common ground, you may discover that the parties seem unmovable at certain points. No one is prepared to budge. At this point take the tack of "reality-tester." With friendly questions, remind the parties of the costs of not settling—the financial cost, the emotional drain, the frustration of on-going hostility, the spiritual loss, etc. Parties in dispute tend to get locked into the immediate competition and forget about long-term costs. Yielding a little further now will probably serve each party far more in the long run. The mediator thus attempts to bring the long-term situation vividly into view.

The long-term view raises a caution also. If the agreed upon solution is to mean anything, both parties must be able to *live with* and *live up to* their end of the agreement. The solution must be genuinely acceptable to both parties. Thus, the mediator must avoid pressuring parties into something they are unready to accept.

What About Outside Resources?

Another possible way to break an impasse is to consider outside resources. Is there a social service, a sympathetic person, a church congregation that could provide the resources necessary to create that common ground? Adding a "slice to the pie" will mean that everyone will come away with more when things are divided up. The parties are used to thinking competitively. Perhaps you can stimulate them to think cooperatively or even do research on your own to uncover additional resources.

Try the Double Column Method

A sometimes more effective variation on "reality-testing" is the "Double Column Method." Ask each party to write in one column all the reasons that favor a particular solution and in another column all the reasons that oppose that solution. When competitiveness predominates and there is much heat but no light, this tactic can help move disputants beyond mere attack and defense towards cooperative problem-solving.

Everyone Must Win

Both parties must feel that they have won something. Otherwise, someone will go home feeling that they have lost and therefore unhappy with the solution. Take for example a case where one neighbor is complaining that the young couple next door plays their stereo at full volume at one a.m. The solution will probably call for a change in behavior of the young couple. But the young couple will be dissatisfied unless they feel that they also have won something in return. *Find* something for them. If nothing else, secure a promise from the complaining party that they will stop complaining. After all, a promise of peace and goodwill is a meaningful win.

An Irrational or Vindictive Fighter

What about those situations where one of the parties seems to be irrational? Someone has lost sight of fairness and a vision of peaceful coexistence. As soon as their opponent yields on one question, they find something else on which to disagree.

This is a recurring problem in conflicts, and a frequent source of failure in dispute resolution. Both parties must genuinely desire peace. There are no easy answers for those situations where both parties are not genuinely committed to resolution. Be prepared for failure.

One suggestion that might help in some situations is to request that the "irrational" party bring with them a trusted friend. When the party makes unfair demands during mediation, their more rational friend will hopefully appeal to reason and good faith while you are caucusing with the other party. Be sure to allow opportunity for the irrational person and their friend to be alone so that this can happen. If you are fortunate enough to see an agreement emerging in this situation, try to get a provision in the agreement that if there are future problems, the parties will discuss their concerns with the friend (or perhaps with you, the mediator) before taking further action. This may discourage the "irrational" party from continually badgering the other party with new demands.

Does This Cover All Crucial Issues?

In most disputes, the mediator will find an area of agreement emerging. After shuttling back and forth two, three, four or more times in caucus, the mediator has worked out an exchange of promises. If the dispute is a complicated one, when you think you've got it settled, go over the issues again with each party separately. What you *don't* want is a situation where you return both parties to the table, outline the agreement they have worked out, and then one party says, "Now, about that other $10,000 you owe me...."

When Agreement Fails

When a dispute has brewed for months or years, a solution may well prove impossible in the first session. Persevere. Several factors frequently reward patience.

1) Parties tend to invest greater trust in the mediator over time. Your influence will grow proportionately.

2) Parties need time to process new information they have heard in the mediation session and soften their attitudes accordingly.

3) Parties may weary of the frustration and expense of continued discord.

4) New events tend to work in favor of compromise and resolution in the presence of a mediator. Other options— litigation, continued hostility, etc.—often look less attractive as time passes if the mediator can maintain communication with both parties.

5) Bitterness and harsh competition are spiritual wounds. Most people need time to open themselves to the healing influence of spiritual faith.

Thus if you come to the end of a two and a half hour session with little or no progress, maintain optimism. See if the parties are willing to continue discussion, either in a meeting scheduled now, or privately with you.

If the parties are agreeable to this, maintain frequent contact with both sides as time elapses. The more contact you have with the parties, usually the greater your effectiveness as a mediator. Make an occasional phone call to see if there are any new developments. Try visiting one or both parties at home—you may find them much more flexible there than in the heat of the first mediation session. Focus discussion on what each party desires and why. What other options are there? What are the long-term pros and cons of the various options?

IV. Agreement

When you have worked out agreement on all issues, summarize the whole agreement, point by point, with both parties present. As a mediator, you have worked hard for that agreement, quite possibly for many hours. Particularly if you have spent a great deal of time in caucus with the parties, it is natural for you to feel pride in achieving resolution and to want recognition for it. Remember that the agreement belongs to the parties. The greater their sense of ownership of what has been hammered out, the greater the likelihood of long-term reconciliation.

Thus, the victory belongs to the former opponents and you are merely summarizing in the presence of both what *they* have worked out. You may wish to present things in this fashion: "Each of you has agreed to do certain things. Mr. Smith, you've agreed to do.... Is that right? Mr. Jones, you've agreed to do.... Is that right?"

Write out the agreement on paper. Agreements not committed to writing have a way of being forgotten, ignored, or misinterpreted. Be specific and clear in writing out the terms—who, what, when, where. Have each party sign the agreement and make a copy for both. Remind them if any difficulties arise in the future you are available to help re-negotiate a new agreement.

Follow-Up

Indicate at the time of the agreement that you will be contacting both parties in the near future to see if they feel the agreement and its implementation are satisfactory. Two to four weeks later is optimum; you may wish to call again six months later. If both parties know that you will retain an interest in their situation, they may be more likely to take seriously their agreement. If problems have arisen you will be in a position to help negotiate a revised agreement.

XI / Structures for Resolving Disputes

Establishing alternative means of dispute resolution is a way both to improve the quality of life within the Christian community as well as to serve others and make visible part of the Christian vision. This chapter describes several forums for resolving disputes. The first section outlines one of the activities of the Mennonite Conciliation Service—a network for resolving disputes among Christians. The second is an example of a much older conflict resolution structure, the "Conciliation Court" supported by the Jewish community in New York City.

The third model described here is that of the "Community Dispute Center," which is attracting increasing interest in the United States today for resolving minor inter-personal disputes. The fourth model describes creative use of reconciliation as an alternative to normal criminal justice processes. The Victim Offender Reconciliation Program was pioneered by Mennonites in Ontario and is now being successfully used in Elkhart, Indiana, in addition to several other communities where local Christians are preparing to establish a similar program.

The MCS Network—Resolving Disputes Among Christians

A family business partnership goes sour. Several members leave the partnership. Others remain and struggle to prevent bankruptcy and foreclosure. With creditors clamoring for money, the remaining members press those who left—now successful in other pursuits—to share responsibility for the old debts. Those who remain refuse on the grounds that they never received compensation for equipment left in the business, nor for a reputation of good craftsmanship built up over many years. The parties prepare to file suit—and counter-suit—in court.

A Christian landlord is charged with inadequate housing maintenance. A group of social workers, many of them also Christians, publicly call him "irresponsible" and release a list of grievances. The landlord denies the charges, points out

*that many of the grievances are petty, and insists he has no
option if he is to serve the community by remodelling houses.
Both sides begin lining up political and legal force to
strengthen their case.*

*Two Christian farmers owned adjoining properties. One
farmer decided to sell housing lots and consequently
changed the path of water drainage. Water now ran with
considerable velocity into the second farmer's field, eroding
his soil. The second farmer complained to friends and made a
few feeble attempts to discuss the situation with his neighbor.
When he received defensive replies, he concluded his
neighbor was determined to avoid changing the situation. He
badgered the county agent to compel his neighbor to adjust
the water flow and began consulting lawyers. The situation
came to a head one day when the teen-age sons of the two
men got into an argument and exchanged blows.*

Through a network of regional contacts, Mennonite Conciliation Service
has been involved in attempting reconciliation in situations such as those
above.

Options for resolving disputes such as these are numerous. In the
dispute involving landlords and social workers, an initial mediation
session was set up involving three mediators acceptable to both sides. After
each side had presented their case, it became clear that the issues were
complex and not easily negotiable. It was agreed to appoint an advisory
mediation panel which would meet periodically with the landlord and the
social workers, to ensure that the social workers could air their concerns
directly, and to allow the landlord opportunity for discussing remodelling
priorities on an on-going basis with tenants and social workers.

The MCS central office received the initial request for assistance in this
case. Both sides agreed in phone calls to meet with mediators, if provided.
The MCS central office located mediators in the area and provided counsel
before the first mediation session. From that point, the local mediators
continued the process.

In the case of the farmers, a local mediator met with each party on
separate occasions, in addition to discussing the situation with the county
agent to gain a better technical understanding. He arranged for a soil
conservation agent to be present at the mediation session in order to
provide perspective on fair expectations from each side, and to suggest
possible solutions.

Both parties were reluctant to meet face-to-face; both were convinced
discussion would be futile. The mediator worked hard to remind both sides
that despite appearances, neither intended harm to the other.

By the time the mediation session occurred, the mediator had a sense for
where some of the misunderstandings had developed and helped to
highlight those incidents. With the air cleared at last, the two neighbors

readily agreed that a solution would require only minor adjustments. It was agreed that the soil conservation agent and the engineer who had designed the drainage system would examine the situation and jointly recommend a solution—which the owner of the development promised to implement.

*　　　*　　　*　　　*　　　*　　　*　　　*

In the case involving a Christian enterprise, the mediator and the parties decided that *arbitration* would be the best solution.

In *mediation*, the parties themselves hammer out a solution, with the mediator serving as a facilitator and go-between. The parties continually modify the proposals under discussion until everyone is satisfied the best solution has been reached.

In *arbitration*, the third-party arbitrators make a decision which both parties have agreed in advance to accept. Both sides make presentations supporting their case. The arbitrators listen and ask questions until they feel satisfied they can make an informed decision. That decision then becomes binding upon both sides.

Usually it is best to attempt mediation first—everyone will be happier if they themselves have had a hand in creating the decision. The only advantage of arbitration is that it guarantees a solution where mediation may fail.

There is an option combining the two alternatives. *Mediation/ arbitration* (known as med/arb) begins by attempting mediation. It is agreed, however, that after a specified number of hours or mediation sessions, if a solution has not been reached, the mediator will become an arbitrator. At that time, he or she proposes a fair solution which becomes binding upon both parties.

A variation on arbitration is *final offer arbitration*. Here each side presents the case to agreed-upon arbitrators as in a normal arbitration procedure. However, instead of the arbitrators producing the solution, each party prepares in writing what he believes to be a fair solution. The arbitrators then select from the two proposals the one they feel to be the fairest. This forces each side to be reasoned and balanced in their proposal—otherwise the opponent's proposal may be selected!

Thus, in this particular business dispute among Christians, mediation was first attempted. Mediation bogged down, however, after several sessions, and one party began preparing for a law suit. After discussing the situation at length with the mediator, however, and being reminded of the tremendous psychological, spiritual, and economic costs of a court battle, the parties agreed to commit themselves to arbitration. Two local business people were selected to join the mediator in forming a three-person arbitration panel.

Each side was asked to summarize on paper their own position. The arbitrators studied the papers in advance and met once with each side to ask additonal questions. In addition to proposing a compromise solution, now binding on both parties, the arbitrators overcame a major obstacle to long-term reconciliation by assisting the family members still running the partnership in consolidating their outstanding debts.

*　　　*　　　*　　　*　　　*　　　*　　　*

The Mennonite Concilation Service, as well as the Christian Conciliation Service, an organization supported by Christian lawyers offering a similar service, is building a network of regional contact people with interest and skill in serving as mediators locally in disputes among Christians. MCS offers training seminars to build skills among people in this network. Requests for mediation or training should be directed to the central MCS office in Akron, Pennsylvania.

Jewish Conciliation Board

Members of the Jewish community in New York City have for decades had recourse to an alternative dispute settlement forum. The Jewish Conciliation Board, established in 1920, is a modern parallel to the ancient Jewish rabbinical courts.[*]

Cases heard in the monthly meetings of the Board vary widely—ranging from disputes between husbands and wives to complaints against Jewish businesspeople to religious conflicts within synagogues.

The purpose of the Conciliation Board, according to James Yaffee's book *So Sue Me!* is four-fold. First, the Board can deal with matters of special Jewish concern that might be incomprehensible to non-Jewish judges. Second, the Board helps to protect the dignity of the Jewish name, by settling disputes privately rather than in public civil proceedings. Thirdly, the Board provides a low-cost and time-saving alternative to court litigation. And fourthly, the Board aims to go beyond dispensing justice to making peace. In the words of one Board member, "We are not going to attempt to say who is morally or legally justified; we are interested in settling things."

Cases are filed by one of the disputing parties with the executive director of the Board at the JCB office. The director discusses the problem with the complaining party at length. If the complaint seems to have substance the director then writes the other party and invites their side of the story. Some cases are resolved at this level with the director serving as conciliator. Those cases remaining unresolved are then scheduled for a hearing before the Board which meets once, occasionally twice, each month.

The Board consists of three volunteers: a rabbi, a lawyer, and a businessperson. The volunteers take turns as Board members and the panel of three may change composition completely from month to month. Additionally, a consulting psychiatrist is present to advise the panel members when needed.

[*]Information and all quotes from *So Sue Me!*, by James Yaffee, Saturday Review Press, 1972

In contrast to the model used in community dispute centers described later in this chapter, the panel members in effect become judges once a case is brought to them. Disputing parties sign an arbitration agreement before the panel will hear the case, binding themselves to accept the judges' decision. Because this agreement is binding and valid before a civil court of law, the Board makes every effort to ensure that nobody signs it unless they really want to. According to Yaffee, "No coercion is used, there is no coaxing, and no special appeal." As a result, not all cases are resolved: "The docket of each session invariably includes two or three cases that never actually come to trial because one party or the other has balked at signing the arbitration agreement." (p. 18)

Sessions are conducted in late afternoon or evening, in informal environment in the conference room of a community building.

The panel members allow each party to present their case in turn, asking clarifying questions throughout. Eventually the panel sends the disputing parties out of the room and confers on a decision. "Many points are likely to be brought up in this conference," Yaffee notes. "Points of common sense, of talmudic law, of practical consequences, of compassion or distrust for the warring parties." Each case is decided on its own merits, not on precedent of previous cases.

"The judges take great care in the wording of their decision," Yaffee observes. "The point must be made in such a way that even the losers, if possible, go off without hard feelings.... There is also an effort...to deal not only with specific issues but with the general principles they embody. The parties to a dispute must ultimately understand the moral implications of what they did." (p. 24)

When possible, the panel gives the disputing parties opportunity to arrive at their own decision rather than impose a decision upon them. Frequently, after presenting their case, parties are asked to retire to another room to work out their own compromise. When they succeed, this agreement becomes the binding recommendation of the judges. When they fail, they are nevertheless more willing to accept the panel's decsion.

"In most cases the parties do find the panel's decision acceptable," Yaffee says. Often the decision precipitates an outburst of emotion. Occasionally there is anger. More frequently, there is happiness—"with everybody apologizing to everybody else and tears flowing freely."

Cases are followed up by the director and volunteer assistants. Sometimes the panel recommends referral of parties to outside resources—the Welfare Department, a marriage counselor, a psychiatrist, or an accountant. In such cases the director makes sure that recommendations are carried out.

Could this model work in other communities as well? Yaffee believes it could. "Other groups," he writes in the concluding paragraph of his book, "might well take the Jewish court as a model for further experiments in community justice. Blacks, chicanos, ethnic minorities, all those who feel intimidated, misunderstood, and betrayed by the 'outside' courts should seriously consider setting up 'conciliation boards' with alterations, of course, to reflect their own values and morals." (p. 269)

Dispute Settlement Centers

— *Two families avoid each other because of a dispute about their common driveway. Matters escalate when the children torment each other at school.*

— *A woman can't sleep at night because of blaring stereos next door. Her neighbors insist that she taunts them with racial slurs.*

— *A landlord demands that tenants pay for plumbing damage he says they caused. The tenants say the bill is exorbitant and unfair.*

What happens in situations such as these, typical in any community? Most would go unsolved, perhaps leading to further hostilities. Those parties wealthy enough might pursue their case in court, where a judge would be forced to render a decision that likely could not take into account the full situation.

In recent years, community-based dispute settlement centers have proved strikingly successful in dealing with disputes such as these.

A small mediation center is established in a rented store front, a church basement or a Legal Services office. Parties in dispute are referred to the center from a variety of sources: social services agencies, police and courts, churches, or self-referral. The complaining party requests a mediation session at the center. The center, often staffed by volunteers, then phones or mails a notice to the other party requesting appearance for mediation. Sometimes disputes are resolved at this level, known as "conciliation," without going to mediation. Sometimes the responding party refuses to cooperate. All told, about 60% of the cases filed in most centers result in a mediation session.

The mediators are volunteers from all walks of life—blue-collar workers, professional people, homemakers, welfare recipients. Each mediator receives 10 to 20 hours of training, mastering the skills of the mediation process in lectures and roleplays. They take cases according to their own schedule, perhaps one case per month, involving 2 to 5 hours.

Mediation sessions are scheduled at a time convenient to both parties, often weekends or Saturdays. The setting is a neutral environment—a conference room at the center, a church, or another community building.

Most centers use a mediation procedure similar to the one presented in Chapter X of this book. Success rates for reaching a mediated agreement vary. A 75% success rate in cases brought to mediation is typical. Follow-up studies at least six months later have shown that more than 80% of mediated agreements remain intact.

Victim/Offender Reconciliation Program*

A Vietnam veteran who had committed a rash of burglaries was imprisoned, but the judge suspended his sentence with the understanding that the offender would make restitution through VORP, the Victim Offender Reconciliation Program.

The offender became a Christian and as he met with his victims, the lives of both were dramatically changed. When the veteran discussed his needs, one victim actually offered the coat off his back; another quoted scripture about forgiveness.

Bringing victim and offender together to discuss the crime committed is the concept of VORP, with which Mennonites in Kitchener, Ontario and Elkhart, Indiana are involved.

When most people think about crime they make a number of common assumptions. After a crime is committed, the proper course is assumed to be a process of judgment and punishment. Guilt must be determined, blame must be placed and the offender must "pay," often by suffering in turn for the suffering he caused; the debt is cancelled when punishment has been carried out.

Responsibility for correcting the wrong brought about by crime is assumed to rest primarily with the state, whose responsibility it is to determine guilt and sentence.

But this view virtually ignores the victim's needs, losses, fears, hostilities and responsibilities. It emphasizes condemnation and rejection of offenders. It does not realize that punishment often fails to correct and in fact is often more destructive than rehabilitative. It is abstract, making people "pay" by suffering rather than by making things right directly to the victim. It is impersonal, leading to stereotypes and bitterness. Participants become pawns, with little say about what happens to them.

This view of the criminal process is also unbiblical. In the biblical view, justice calls for a restoration of right relationships, of a "making things right" directly to the person harmed. The Hebrew word for restitution as used in the Old Testament is based on the same root word as "shalom," the biblical idea of peace combined with well-being and right relationships. Restitution thus involves making peace, "giving back" in order to restore health to persons and relationships.

In the New Testament we are called upon to love unconditionally, to forgive and to accept, to reconcile rather than to condemn and accuse. Clearly, our usual assumptions need to be re-examined.

Thus an alternative view is to recognize that crime involves conflict between people which ruptures right relationships within the community. Relationships cannot be resolved simply by punishing the offender

*By Howard Zehr, VORP director in Elkhart, Indiana. Reprinted courtesy of MCC News Service.

without dealing with underlying feelings of bitterness and enmity which will inevitably remain on both sides. The problem is not simply the offender's or the physical damage caused. Both sides need to take part in finding a solution. Since it involves the life of the community, the community needs to particpate as well; responsibility cannot simply be handed over to the state.

Needed are opportunities for reconciliation, channels by which participants can explore the feelings, questions and misunderstandings that inevitably emerge after a crime. and avenues by which they can participate in the decision about how to make it right. We often confine our thinking to global terms, failing to recognize the opportunities for peacemaking at home,not seeing that the solution to crime involves peacemaking.

The victim-offender reconciliation concept, originally pioneered by Mennonite Central Committee in Ontario but now operating with Mennonite involvement in such areas as Elkhart, Indiana and Winnipeg, Manitoba attempts to embody this view uniquely and straightforwardly.

Victims and offenders who agree to participate are brought together to meet and talk. Trained community volunteers, not professional criminal justice agents representing the state, arrange and mediate encounters. In these meetings, opportunity is provided for both sides to express the feelings that hinder reconciliation, to ask the questions that have been bothering them, to agree upon what happened and what should be done about it, to negotiate their own settlement (usually in the form of a restitution contract) rather than having a settlement imposed by the state.

It is a simple concept—yet the implications are profound, and the results sometimes dramatic. Stereotypes break down, hostilities are worked out, restitution contracts agreed upon. The lives of victims and offender are often altered, sometimes dramatically, as reconciliation occurs.

Clearly the victim-offender reconciliation process cannot always work and may not be suitable for all crimes. Nor does it solve basic problems of injustice within the criminal justice process. However, it can work and is a step in the right direction.

And it is a step in which it is vitally important that we be involved. Victim-offender reconciliation is a kind of practical peacemaking, a way of putting our belief in peace and reconciliation to work in our own communities.

Conflict
in the
Group

Jesus was not passive in conflict. "In the Sermon on the Mount he said that when you have been struck on one cheek you should turn the other cheek. What that means to me is that when the battle has begun, I do not leave, nor do I attack. I stay there. I stay in range of getting hit again. I take the risk of not destroying the person or leaving the scene."

"If the members of your congregation don't have some sense of hope about being able to work out a solution, then people end up feeling they must either be doormats, or drive those who disagree out of the organization. Often these attitudes are not thought out or stated quite as boldly as I have put them here, but their presence is revealed in the style of the battle as it is joined."

"I have not worked in a congregation yet where from an outside perspective, one 'side' was blameless. In every case each group has participated to a greater or lesser degree in blaming the other for the problems. Further, each group sees itself as much more benevolent toward the other than it actually is.... If each group is willing to look seriously at how it causes, creates, or adds to the organizational difficulty, not only will the conflict diminish, but there is greater possibility that an agreement may be reached."

"I will make the assumption that if we work at it long enough we will find a way to work things out between us. This is a faith statement; it is a statement of hope. Any relationship presupposes a commitment to a joint outcome, an agreement that each partner may have to give up a little in order to reach a solution both can live with."

  —Speed Leas in
   A Lay Person's Guide to Conflict Management(Alban Institute)

XII / A Framework for Managing Group Conflict

Repeatedly I have observed that individuals in a group struggling with conflict feel burdened, not so much by the difficulties of any one task, but by an overall sense of uncertainty and unpredictability. *What should we do next? Is there such a thing as a resolution process? How do we link that into what's happening here?* What follows is an effort to impose some order on the uncertainties of a group conflict, such as a congregational dispute. Many of the practical suggestions offered here are drawn from an excellent little manual entitled *Church Fights* by Speed Leas and Paul Kittlaus (Westminster, 1973).

No, a conflict resolution process functioning in reality will not be nearly so tidy as the one that unfolds neatly on the following pages. The goal here is not to provide a universal recipe accounting for everything that happens in group conflicts, but rather to stake out general orientation points and some practical suggestions for the group or leader groping for next moves in conflict.

As with any complex task, conflict is much easier managed when broken down into a series of smaller assignments. Three small chores are not nearly so formidable as one huge problem with neither a recognizable head nor tail. *Tackle the beast in three stages: 1) the Contract Stage; 2) the Problem Definition Stage; 3) the Problem Resolution Stage.*

I. Agree on a Contract

Members of the Nurture Committee at the Tall Oaks Community Church began advocating formation of small fellowship groups. Instead of the usual Sunday evening service, they proposed that the congregation meet in small groups in homes. Strongly differing opinions quickly surfaced within the congregation as word of the discussion reached others. Tensions about charismatic issues already present and never discussed immediately surfaced as well and fueled the disagreement. Although the Nurture Committee was not yet prepared to make a proposal, the topic of small groups was raised at the next congregational meeting. Angry opinions were offered from several viewpoints. After ten minutes of heated discussion, the minister suddenly arose and announced that the issue was too divisive and should be indefinitely tabled. The meeting

was adjourned and the Nurture Committee dropped its discussion.
Three months later, the minister resigned.

The "Contract Stage" is crucial in managing conflict. The group above was moving into the Contract Stage, but got stopped dead in its tracks. Instead of dealing openly and positively with the presence of disagreement, and setting in motion a process for resolving it, the group was forced to ignore disagreement. The result was tension too high for the minister to tolerate and a severe set-back in congregational morale and cooperation which lingered several years.

Why A Contract is Important

Pay careful attention to the Contract Stage, and your group will stand a good chance of coming to satisfactory resolution of its problems. Three important things happen in this first stage of resolving a conflict: 1) *The presence of conflict moves into open discussion.* Perhaps a portion of an ordinary congregational business meeting is devoted to discussion of the conflict. Or a special meeting is convened to consider the problem. The point is that now the group acknowledges openly that a problem exists that must be tackled. 2) *A common understanding, a framework for proceeding, is created about the next steps for tackling the problem.* This framework will provide the basis for moving ahead in the midst of disagreements. 3) *The group gains momentum towards cooperation by tackling the very manageable and practical questions of procedure first.*

There is no need for all this to happen in one meeting. What *is* important is the direction the group is moving—*towards* conflict, not away. The presence of conflict must move from the shadows into the light if a contract is to be formed.

If nothing more can be accomplished, at least agree on a time and place to discuss the disagreement further. Had the minister above suggested that the issues are numerous and complex, and perhaps a committee should be appointed to examine them, the congregation could have acted on its difficulties. Even a suggestion to set aside one hour in the next congregational meeting would have kept things moving in the right direction. Instead, the conflict was pushed underground, only to reappear in various forms for several years thereafter.

What Does the Contract Include?

"Contract" here does not necessarily mean a formal agreement couched in lawyers' language. Rather it means an informal understanding within the group about next steps. Leas and Kittlaus suggest four areas which a group should discuss and agree on when developing their contract: the *process,* the *decision rule, goals,* and the *timeline.* Use a blackboard and summarize the group's decision in each of these areas.

Agree on the Process

Decide first of all as a group how to proceed. What will happen next? Who will do it? How will they do it? To whom will they report? And after that?

The more specifically the group can outline the process now, the more manageable the issues in dispute will be.

The process part of your contract might look something like this:

> We will begin by requesting both groups to present their case uninterrupted in a congregational meeting.

> Second, we will provide a time for clarifying questions after each side has presented their case. We will not debate the issues until each group is satisfied that others understand their viewpoint.

> Third, we will try to define the problems in a statement that all can agree with.

> Then we will discuss options for resolving the problems and vote on the best strategy.

> We will break into small discussion groups for defining the problem and brainstorming for solutions.

> We will be honest in our opinions but try to state them in a spirit of Christian love.

There are other things which might be included in the contract. What about inviting a referee to serve as a facilitator in the process at some point? Does the group wish to delegate certain information-gathering tasks to a selected committee? How about appointing a "task force" with representatives from both sides to examine certain options for resolution in detail or to bring recommendations to the whole group?

Agree on the Decision Rule

Agree on how you will make decisions as part of your contract discussion and you will find it easier later to make decisions and live with them. *Consensus decision-making* is excellent, but it takes time. *Voting* by simple majority is fast, but many groups discover that a decision made by this method can be difficult to live with later—frequently a group of significant size is voted down and remains dissatisfied.

A good compromise is to use the vote for decisions but to set the required percentage of votes high. If a 70% or even 80% affirmative vote is required, most any decision will command the discussion and accommodation necessary for long-term support.

Agree On Goals

Discuss and list general goals in the contract stage as a way of affirming what all members hold in common. Example (from a church disagreeing on how to conduct community outreach):

> We wish to be open to what God desires for us.
> We would like to experience reconciliation in Christ.
> We wish to be a group which has room for people of differing viewpoints.
> We believe we are called to share the Good News.
> We would like to find a way to evangelize in which everyone in our church can participate.

Agree on a Time Line

Decide on a time line in order to prevent the conflict resolution process from getting sidetracked or filibustered. One of the "laws of conflict" is that people will avoid making a decision as long as they can possibly do so. An agreed-upon time line helps prevent this. Perhaps more important, it provides an atmosphere of manageability. Conflict is less threatening when everyone knows it will not drag on forever!

II. Define the Problem

A church found itself caught in disagreement over charismatic worship. After months of growing and ill-camouflaged tension, a meeting was called to air concerns. The highpoint of the meeting came when the leader of one faction threatened to take his group elsewhere. Within minutes, the minister hinted at resigning and the head of the Board of Elders suggested that maybe it was time that the church developed a covenant which all members would sign. This comment triggered a long, heated argument about who was delaying the covenant process. At 11:30 p.m. the group disbanded, more divided and confused than when they met.

A school board met to discuss recent allegations of racism. In that meeting, one board member stated angrily that he had been calling for a Black Studies Program for years and now he intended to publicly announce his support for such a program. Another member presented an outline for a cross-cultural learning center which several parents had given to him. The board chairman allowed that he thought they should bring in consultants from the state. By the end of the evening, the board was split in three factions and unable to agree on anything except the need for further discussion.

The most common error in resolving conflicts is failure to begin by first defining the problem. The groups above were "solution-oriented" instead of problem-oriented. They started wrongly by discussing solutions first, which of course were manifold. With no agreement on what the solutions were intended to solve, confusion and division only increased as discussion heated up around the merits of the various proposed solutions.

The best way to find solutions to conflict is to *begin by defining the problem.* Sometimes a group can abbreviate the Contract Stage, but there are no short-cuts in the Problem-Defining Stage. Only when your group can agree specifically on the problems at hand are you ready to discuss solutions constructively. Normally that means being able to say *who* is doing (or not doing), *what* (to whom, if applicable), *when* (or where).

Get the Information You Need

Before you can define the problem, you need accurate information about the various viewpoints and expectations within the group. There are a variety of ways to do this. The simplest, of course, is to *convene a meeting* in which individuals or groups are able to state their concerns. In many ways, this is just an ordinary old "gripe session." But there are two big differences. One is that careful attention is given to seeing that all viewpoints are heard, not just those of the bold or of the majority viewpoint. Second, at some point in this meeting or in a sequel, a concerted effort is made to state gripes in such a way that: 1) something can be done about them; and 2) the group can agree on which are the most pressing problems.

If the conflict is not complex and the group not large, one session may be adequate to gather information and define the problem. But what about situations where isseus are complex, the group is large, resentment is high, and individuals are reluctant to speak their concerns openly?

In such circumstances, information-gathering must be structured in a way that allows all viewpoints to be heard. Leas and Kittlaus suggest several data-gathering instruments for this purpose.

Develop A Questionnaire

One is a *questionnaire*. Questions may be open-ended ("I think the greatest problem facing our church is   .") Or scaled-response("I think the minister's sermons are: poor — passable — excellent.") Or multiple choice.

Regardless how you structure it, two things are crucial if you use a questionnaire for gathering information. One, be sure that all factions are involved in designing, implementing and evaluating the questionnaire. Otherwise there may be charges the whole thing is rigged. Second, share the results of the questionnaire at a time and place when all factions can be present. If possible, agree in advance during the Contract Stage where and how the data will be shared.

Conduct Interviews

Another means of gathering information is *interviews*. Leas and Kittlaus offer several suggestions here. For one, interviewers should be neutral parties in the conflict—bring in an outsider if necessary. For another, interviewers should assure those they meet with that all information will be used anonymously—no names will be revealed at any time.

When comes the time to report the results of interviews, categorize findings, but use verbatim feed-back generously to illustrate each category. Quotes such as "We simply don't have the physical space to do the things we would like to with the youth group." are much more effective than simply reporting that ten people believe the church should add a new wing.

Finally, before sharing results of interviews with the whole group, inform all key people about what will be shared, as a way of building confidence with them. Hold a small meeting with leaders of each faction, the pastor, and any other key leaders in the group.

Plan Small Group Discussion

The third and probably the best way of gathering information is *small group discussion*. This method is fast and flexible. Perhaps most important, group discussion is participatory. Properly structured, group participation almost always helps change the atmosphere from a fight climate to a problem-solving climate.

You may wish to convene small groups at separate times and then report from each small group back to the larger group. Or you may wish to call a large meeting and then break down into small randomly-formed groups as a part of that meeting. However you do it, you will need to provide the small groups with some tasks to generate and focus discussion. How about one of the following?

Have each member make a drawing or collage representing the larger group and then explain it to fellow members of the sub-group.

Have small groups develop a brief questionnaire which each member fills out. Discuss results in the small group and then share them with the larger group.

Have small groups draw a time line of the significant events of the conflict up to the present. Return to large group and have representatives from each small group jointly draw one large time line.

Have each sub-group draw a chart showing the centers of power. Begin with one large circle representing the whole group, and then place smaller circles within, each corresponding in size to the group they represent, and overlapping with others at appropriate points. Miller and King, for example, may be members both of the church council as well as of the group opposed to building a new church wing.

Feed the Information Back

The point of data-gathering is to get all relevant opinions and desires into the open so that the group can proceed with finding solutions. Thus, no matter how you have gone about gathering data, the next step is to present the information to the whole group. Use a neutral person who summarizes the findings before the entire body. Or have representatives from the small group report into the large group when you have reconvened. Or have each small group place a summary of their discussion on newsprint.

Leas and Kittlaus state well what should happen in the feed-back session: "The key here is that the situation gets stated and restated over and over again, first in one kind of jargon and then in another until everyone has a common understanding of the same problems." (page 107). Be sure to allow time for discussion, modifications, and additions in this session!

Define the Problem in "Workable Problem Statements"

You've gathered a wide variety of desires and opinions. You've brought this data back to the group. Now you must organize the data in such a way that the group can do something about it. This is the task of defining the problems.

How you state the problems is crucial. Write them out. Make them specific—one sentence for each problem ought to suffice. A good problem definition contains three and preferably four of the following: *who*, is doing (or not doing) *what*, to *whom*, *when* (or *where*). Here is a list of problem statements created by one church after several data-gathering sessions.

> *The Pastoral Search Committee does not have a list of specific criteria for the selection of candidates that has been approved by the whole church.*

> *The members of the church youth group feel that they are not allowed to make their own decisions as to who the youth group leader should be and as to what they will do and discuss at their meetings.*

> *The chairmen of all the church committees do not have enough skill or understanding of small-group leadership and how to do problem-solving efficiently.* (Leas and Kittlaus, p. 151)

Having stated the difficulties in these problem statements, the church was able to move easily through a problem-solving process. *Clear problem statements are crucial to finding good solutions.*

III. Solve the Problem

When you have heard concerns and have cast them in the form of "workable problem statements," you are ready to create solutions.

Set Priorities

Begin by prioritizing the problems. Which demand immediate solutions or lengthy discussion? Often it is wise to settle the easy problems first, to establish a cooperative mood. For the same reason, if you will be deciding general policy questions as well as specific cases affected by policy, undertake the general policy issues first. For example, decide first on the church's policies for funding local projects before wading into the tangle between supporters of the day care center and the food coop over church dollars.

State Criteria for Good Solutions

If tension is high or a problem complex, a helpful way to initiate cooperation is to list the characteristics of a good solution before discussing solutions. For example:

> *A good solution would:*

> *1) Fulfill the needs of those desiring more contemporary worship forms.*

> *2) Assure others that the church maintains commitment to traditional forms of worship.*

> *3) Keep the minister better informed of feelings of both groups.*

Task Forces for Complex Issues

When problems require considerable research, assigning a task group may be the best way to explore solutions. Be sure to include members of the various opposing factions. A task force will operate with much greater clarity if it begins its work by stating its objectives. Leas and Kittlaus suggest the following:

> Who will do the job.
> What specific action they will take.
> When they will complete their task.
> The extent to which the job will be done.
> Who will be affected. (p. 153)

Generate Solutions

Whether you discuss solutions in task forces or as a large group, it is important to have a variety of solutions before you. *Brainstorming* is a proven tactic for this.

The method is to set aside a time period in which as many solutions as possible are listed, ranging from the practical to the absurd. Work in small groups to set an atmosphere of freedom and informality. Evaluation and research will come later—for now have fun making the list a long one. The resulting flow of creativity often yields ideas useful in fashioning the final solution.

When the group has developed a list of possible solutions, take a break. Let the ideas incubate. When you return, add new ones that might have occurred.

Choose the Most Feasible

From this abundance of ideas, discard the obviously impossible. Then select the several most feasible and discuss or research each. Finally, after you have examined these, select or create the best solution.

Implementation and Review

Obviously, when a strategy for solution has been agreed upon, it needs to be presented to the full group for approval and implementation. Take the occasion to review the process and consider what the group has learned about responding to conflict.

Any group which works through the stages of contract-formation, problem-defining, and problem-solving accomplishes much more than resolving one conflict. A group learns a great deal about honesty, mutuality, and decision-making by seeing a conflict through to resolution. Having faced one conflict successfully, a group will be much stronger in future conflicts. What has your group learned that will be helpful in future decision-making and group relations?

XIII / Facilitating Group Discussion

Constructive discussion is basic to resolving conflicts in groups. Skilled **discussion facilitators** *are key to constructive discussion. I have seen a good facilitator create an almost electric sense of free exchange and discovery in a group by nourishing good-natured dissent and deftly summarizing the direction of the discussion periodically, without imposing her own opinions on the group. I have also seen an inept facilitator put a group to sleep by rambling on with his own viewpoints for most of the time allotted.*

The following suggestions speak to a variety of situations. They were originally developed for use in a church setting where ordination of women was at issue. Leaders planned a one-day discussion conference consisting of papers presented from several viewpoints, interspersed with small group discussion. Discussion facilitators received notice well in advance and met for a 45-minute orientation to their task at the beginning of the day.

I. Beginning

A. **Physical Arrangements**

1) Chalkboard or newsprint handy?
2) Can everyone see each other?
3) Room temperature and ventilation.

B. **Introductions**

1) Have each person introduce self or an adjacent person, if size allows.
2) Learn names as quickly as you can.

C. **Assistants**

1) A time keeper to remind of half-way point or of time allotted to each discussion item?
2) A recorder to list on the board key issues and responses of the group on each?

D. **Focus Discussion.** If only one item, state the topic briefly. If several, summarize and list them on the board.

II. During

A. **Mood.** Keep discussion informal and spirits high. Encourage ease, good humor, and enjoyment of free exchange. Receive all statements openly and with respect. "Disapproval kills discussion, disagreement stimulates it."

B. **Keep discussion focused.** Listen with appreciation to all ideas, but stress issues at hand. Without being legalistic about it, try to maintain focus on one issue at a time. List other issues on the board for subsequent discussion as they are raised. If attention strays to personalities, return it to issues.

C. When issues are complex or emotions high, **use the board frequently.** *Translating opinions into print* as they are offered helps set a rational atmosphere. Likewise, if you *list issues as they are raised,* it makes it easier to restrict discussion to one issue at a time and to remain issue-centered rather than personality-centered.

D. **Summarize occasionally,** perhaps every 10 minutes. "Let's see where we've been going...." Summarize the various opinions as fairly and accurately as you can.

E. **Encourage input from all.** "Let's have some discussion on this question...." "What do others have to say on this...?" Avoid putting individuals on the spot with a question directed specifically to one person, unless you can see an idea struggling to find words there already: "Bob, were you going to say something here...?"

   Interrupt the "speechmaker" as tactfully as you can. "While we're on this, let's hear from some of the others." " Can we hear some other opinions on this one...?"

F. **Keep your own views out of the discussion** as much as you can. Yes, your opinions count, too, and sometimes merit a place in the discussion. But your first responsibility is to help others get their ideas out by listening well and asking clarifying questions. Aim to be neutral, though not detached.

H. · **If a strongly-worded opinion threatens the group's sense of tolerant exchange, summarize the opinion in more rational terms,** laundered of emotion. "Mr. Brown is saying he believes.... What other opinions are there on this point?"

I. **Clarify language differences.** Are individuals using the same word with several different meanings?

III. Ending

A. **Emphasize points of discovery or agreement.**

B. **Summarize unresolved areas,** restating opposing viewpoints as fairly as possible. **Nourish interest** in continuing study and discussion.

C. If **further activity** is planned, be sure there is clarity about who, what, when, etc.

Guide to Further Resources

The following represent a small portion of a rapidly growing body of literature and a proliferating field of groups working in dispute resolution. For further reading suggestions or guidelines to active agencies, see bibliographies in the following books or contact Mennonite Conciliation Service.

Literature

Mediation: A Reader, edited by Ron Kraybill and Lynn Buzzard, director of the Christian Legal Society, 1980. Articles and essays on conflict mediation. Extensive bibliography and guide to other resources 15 pages in length. Aimed at Christians, outlining parameters of the field and establishing the scriptural mandate for Christian involvement in conflict ministries. $8.50 (order from MCC).

"Conflict Resolution: A Challenge for the Church." *Engage/Social Action* magazine, 1978. Articles by James Laue and John Adams, with five brief case examples and list of resources for training, research, and intervention. 40¢ per copy (order from MCC) 40 pages.

At the Heart of the Whirlwind, by John P. Adams. (Harper & Row), 1976. Absorbing accounts by a veteran conflict intervenor, a United Methodist reverend. Focuses on civil rights struggles, in addition to Kent State, Wounded Knee, and the 1971 Miami Beach political convention. $6.95 (order from publisher) 146 pages.

Church Fights: Managing Conflict in the Local Church by Speed Leas and Paul Kittlaus. (Westminster Press), 1973. Step-by-step format, outlining strategy from beginning to end for congregational conflicts. $7.95 (order from publisher) 186 pages.

A Lay Person's Guide to Conflict Management, by Speed Leas. (The Alban Institute, Mt. St. Alban, Washington, D.C. 20016), 1979. Causes of congregational conflict and suggestions for managing it. $2.50 (order from MCC or publisher) 15 pages.

International Mediation: Ideas for the Practitioner by Roger Fisher. (International Peace Academy, 777 United Nations Plaza, New York City, NY 10017), 1978. Written for international conflicts but also valuable for inter-group community disputes. Well organized in a trouble-shooting style. Practical and packed with useful ideas. $10.00 plus $2.00 for handling (order from publisher) 159 pages.

Mediating the Victim/Offender Conflict by Howard Zehr. (Mennonite Central Committee), 1980. Introduces use of mediation as an alternative in criminal justice. Includes case study, rationale, and process description. 50¢ (order from MCC) 24 pages.

The Use of Out-of-Court Means for Resolving Indian Conficts. (Indian Law Resource Center, 601 E Street, S.E., Washington, D.C. 20003), 1980. An example of the many creative uses alternative dispute resolution processes are finding. Presents over-view of history of Indian rights, court litigation and the need for alternatives. Good introduction to the various dispute resolution processes available. 100 pages.

Alternative Methods of Dispute Settlement: A Selected Bibliography compiled by Frank E. A. Sauder and Frederick E. Snyder. Available free from: Special Committee on Resolution of Minor Disputes, American Bar Association, 1800 M Street, N.W., Washington, D.C. 20036. 54 pages.

"A Guide to Peace Resources." Two-page guide with 100 entries on such topics as "Biblical Studies," "Periodicals," "Peace Organizations," "Study Guides," etc. Free from MCC.

Organizations

Christian Conciliation Service, P.O. Box 2069, Oak Park, IL 60303. Recently formed service of the Christian Legal Society, a network of evangelical lawyers. Provides Christian lawyers as mediators or arbitrators in several metropolitan areas nationwide. Developing literature and training resources.

Community Conflict Resolution Program, Center for Metropolitan Studies, University of Missouri, St. Louis, MO 63121. Contact: James H. Laue, Director. (216) 672-3143. University program headed by an active churchman with formidable experience as a pioneer in community dispute intervention and training.

Community Relations Service, U.S. Department of Justice, 550 11th Street, N.W., Washington, D.C. 20530. Provides assistance in disputes nationwide with racial aspects.

Institute for Mediation and Conflict Resolution, 46 E. 68th Street, New York, NY 20530. Contact: George Nicolau. Intervention and broad training experience.

Mennonite Conciliation Service, Akron, PA 17501. (717) 859-1151. See below.

Ron Kraybill has been director of the Mennonite Conciliation Service since its beginning in 1979. He concentrated in conflict resolution while a student at Goshen College, Associated Mennonite Biblical Seminaries, and Harvard Divinity School. In 1980 he co-edited with Lynn Buzzard **Mediation: A Reader.**

The Mennonite Conciliation Service is a service of the Mennonite Central Committee U.S. Peace Section, which is supported by the Mennonite and Brethren in Christ churches. Through its central coordinator in Akron, Pennsylvania, and a growing network of Christians nationwide, MCS assists in resolving disputes among Christians and in the communities in which they live.